DELICIOUS RECIPES *for* HEALTHY LIVING

grain-free

GOURMET

JODI BAGER *and* JENNY LASS

Dear Judith,
thanks for always
going out of your way
to feed me things I
can eat!
love,
Jenny

GRAIN-FREE · REFINED-SUGAR-FREE · LOW-LACTOSE

whitecap

Edited by Elaine Jones
Proofread by Nelles Hamilton
Design by Diane Yee
Photography by Joseph Marranca
Fine Pressware Ceramics by Kosby & Bouchard
Recipe on cover: Gourmet Pizza

The authors would like to thank Maureen Greenstein for their makeup.

Printed and bound in Canada

Library and Archives Canada Cataloguing in Publication

Lass, Jenny
    Grain-free gourmet / Jenny Lass, Jodi Bager.

Includes index.
ISBN 1-55285-668-2

    1. Gluten-free diet—Recipes. I. Bager, Jodi II. Title.

RM237.86.L38 2005   641.5'638   C2005-903038-0

The publisher acknowledges the financial support of the Government of Canada through the Book Publishing Industry Development Program for our publishing activities.

Dedication

JODI—To my devoted husband, Steven, and children, Sam and Theo, who are my reasons for getting well and staying well; and to Elaine Gottschall, who, through her life's work, enabled me to do so.

JENNY—To my parents, Diana and Harold, for their unending support; to Helen Byrt for introducing me to the world of writing and continuing to guide me through it; and to Elaine Gottschall for saving my life.

Acknowledgements

I thank my parents, Wendy and Elliott Eisen, and Punny and Jill Litwack for their love and encouragement, advice and support. Thank you to my sisters, Tammy, Robin, and Jennifer, and their husbands, Paul, Bill, and Bob, who eagerly sampled creations and encouraged new ones. My friends endured countless meals and taste tests whether they were hungry or not; I thank them for that. Thank you to Lougie Ang for her willingness to taste anything and clean up everything. I am so grateful to my dear friend Krista Thompson, who first introduced me to the Specific Carbohydrate Diet, which changed my life. And finally, this book would not have been written without Jenny Lass, whose research and writing expertise are as invaluable as her partnership.

Jodi Bager

I thank my parents, Harold and Diana, who changed the way they eat so I could be well. Thanks to my friends and family, who are always willing to taste my experiments and accommodate my fussy stomach when we have meals together. Thank you Judy and Jane Macijauskas and Tanya Spiegelberg for your honest opinions and making the Wasaga Burger famous. Thanks to Helen Byrt for fostering my career and letting me use her office as a writing haven. Thank you to Kala Solway, who introduced me to the Specific Carbohydrate Diet, and to Dr. Christina Fisher, who has always supported me being on the SCD. I also thank Jodi Bager, whose valued partnership, countless generous snacks and meals, and proficiency in all things fish made this book possible.

Jenny Lass

The authors would like to thank AnnMarie MacKinnon, Elaine Jones, Alison Maclean, Helen Stortini, Trent Olson, and Whitecap Books for their hard work, support, and faith in this project. We would also like to thank Malcolm Lester for his guidance, and Fiona Press, Helen Byrt, and Alisa Vickers for making sure our science is sound. Thank you to Joseph Marranca, a most talented photographer, for the beautiful photographs in this book; and to Michelle Kosoy for lending us her elegant ceramics for these photographs. Thanks also to Maureen Greenstein for making us look presentable. When you write a cookbook, many sources inspire you. From trying new combinations in restaurants to watching cooking shows, you discover that your desire to create finds fuel in every taste and technique.

To that end, we acknowledge the following people and sources that inspired us: Lougie Ang, Judith and Norman Bager, Mark Bittman, Elena Cardenas, Robyn Codas, Violet Currie, Karin Digout, Selma Eisen, Wendy and Elliott Eisen, Elaine Elliot, epicurious.com, Carol Frilegh, Beverley and Peter Gold, Elaine Gottschall, Maureen Greenstein, Kim and Tom Hansen, W.B. Herman, John Higgins, the Jaye family, Sue and Tanya Krivel, Lois Lang, Harold and Diana Lass, Virginia Lee, Carrie Lehman, Punny and Jill Litwack, Gillian and John Marshall, Anna Olson, Rose Reisman, Randy Rosen, Monda Rosenberg, Lucy Rosset, Sharon Sobel, Kay Spicer, SuzyQ, Anat and Illy Taiber, Yossi and Tami Tanuri, Lucy Waverman, and Lani Zigelstein.

Disclaimer

The food in this book isn't intended to be a substitute for medication prescribed to you, or for the advice of a qualified physician, dietitian, or other health professional. Always consult with a physician if you have any health problems, such as high cholesterol, low bone density, or chronic diarrhea. You should also consult your physician before changing your diet. The health information in this book was researched and documented by the authors to the best of their ability, and was current at the time of manuscript submission. The naming of any product in this book doesn't imply endorsement by the authors or the publisher.

Table of Contents

INTRODUCTION

Food takes you on a journey. The comfort you get from just the right taste and texture satisfies more than your hunger. Food has the power to make the world seem perfect—at least for those few moments when you're savouring your favourite meal or dessert. But for people who try to adjust what they eat in an effort to be healthier, mealtime can become a chore rather than a pleasure. Fortunately, you don't have to abandon the dishes you love if you're on a specialized diet.

We first met when driving together to a potluck lunch for people who follow the Specific Carbohydrate Diet (SCD). This diet, developed by Dr. Sydney Valentine Haas and made famous by Elaine Gottschall, has helped thousands of people with intestinal problems, including those with autism, to eliminate or control their debilitating symptoms. During the drive to the potluck, we discussed our respective routes from severe illness—celiac disease and ulcerative colitis—to improved health through the SCD. We also started sharing recipes—what we made and how we made it, both of us incredulous at how our revised dishes tasted better than the originals. Over the course of the next few months, we realized that our passion for experimenting and creating in the kitchen had led us both to gather a repertoire of signature dishes that were more than just healthy and delicious; they were well worth sharing. This book is the convergence of these two paths: good health and a love of cooking, followed by two grateful women whose lives were saved by eating this food.

In this cookbook, we re-introduce you to your favourite meals, with a twist; all of our recipes are grain-free and refined-sugar-free, and contain little or no lactose. Our secret ingredient is ground almonds, also called almond flour. This grain substitute is perfect for anyone who has lactose or gluten intolerance, low calcium intake, high cholesterol, or an intestinal disease—or simply for anyone who loves delicious, nutritious food. We show you cooking tricks that will improve your health, fool your taste buds, and amaze your dinner guests.

We hope you enjoy these recipes and discover new favourites that will keep you happy and healthy for years to come.

NOTES FROM
THE KITCHEN: THE BASICS

These recipes were developed to be not only healthy but also healing. Some of the ingredients we use have unique properties that can help lower your cholesterol and improve and maintain your intake of fibre, vitamins, minerals, and protein. In this section, you'll find out about some of the key ingredients in our recipes: how to use them, where to find them, and why they're important.

Almond Flour—That's Nuts!

At first, substituting ground or powdered almonds for grains may seem—excuse the pun—nuts. But there are good reasons for this switch.

- **Almond flour helps your heart.** More and more research shows that almonds are good for your heart. In fact, in one study, almonds significantly lowered LDL (the "bad" cholesterol) and increased HDL (the "good" cholesterol) when research participants were fed almond-flour muffins like the ones in this book. Almonds even outshone the LDL cholesterol-lowering action of whole wheat.

- **Almond flour can be easier to digest.** Many people with sensitive intestines tolerate almond flour better than grains. A 2004 physician-run survey of patients with inflammatory bowel disease found that the Specific Carbohydrate Diet, which uses almond flour as a grain substitute, helped 84% of participants achieve remission—61% of the patients were off all medications.

- **Almond flour is nutritious.** Almond flour has a lot of vitamins and minerals that all-purpose wheat flour doesn't. For example, 85 g (3 oz) of almonds—about 75 nuts—give you 105% of your daily recommended vitamin E intake (see chart page opposite). Almond flour also has more calcium, which is important for healthy bones, teeth, nerves, muscles, and blood. Almonds provide natural calcium without the gas, bloating, and diarrhea that can sometimes come from eating dairy products (see chart below).

Nutritional Content for 1 oz (28 g) Almonds* Calories: 160 Calories from fat: 120		
Nutrient	**Amount**	**% Daily Value**** (n/a=not applicable)
Total Fat	14 g	22%
Monounsaturated	9 g	n/a
Polyunsaturated	3.5 g	n/a
Saturated	1 g	n/a
Cholesterol	0 mg	n/a
		Continued on next page

Nutritional Content for 1 oz (28 g) Almonds* (continued)		
Nutrient	**Amount**	**% Daily Value** (n/a=not applicable)
Total Carbohydrate	6 g	2%
Dietary Fibre	3 g	12%
Protein	6 g	n/a
Sugars	1 g	n/a
Vitamins and Minerals		
Vitamin E		35%
Folate		4%
Calcium		8%
Iron		20%
Magnesium		6%
Phosphorus		15%
Potassium	200 mg	6%
Sodium	0 mg	n/a

*Source: Almond Nutrition Facts. Almond Board of California, 2003.

**Percent daily values are based on a 2,000-calorie diet.

- **Almond flour is a good source of fibre.** Although almond flour can be gentler than grains on a sensitive digestive system, it's high in fibre. Just 85 g (3 oz) of almonds supply 36% of your daily value of dietary fibre (see chart to left).

- **Almond flour is satisfying.** Because almonds are high in protein and mono-unsaturated fat (that's the "good" fat), they satisfy your appetite longer than carbohydrates (see chart to left).

- **Almond flour tastes great.** Most people can't tell the difference between our dishes made with almond flour and their dishes made with wheat flour. We've found that most of the time almond flour is a better wheat substitute than rice, spelt, or potato flour in terms of taste and texture.

Calcium in Selected Foods*

Recommended daily intake of calcium:
Age 4 to 8 = 800 mg
Age 9 to 18 = 1,300 mg
Age 19 to 50, and pregnant or lactating women
  18+ = 1,000 mg
Age 50+ = 1,500 mg

Food	Amount	Calcium (mg)
Almonds	½ cup (125 mL)	200
Bok choy, cooked	1 cup (250 mL)	163
Broccoli, cooked	½ cup (125 mL)	38
Cheese		
Brie	2 oz (50 g)	92
Brick, Cheddar, Colby, Edam and Gouda	2 oz (50 g)	350
Camembert	2 oz (50 g)	194
Parmesan, grated	3 Tbsp (45 mL)	261
Swiss	2 oz (50 g)	480

Calcium in Selected Foods* (continued)

Food	Amount	Calcium (mg)
Lentils, cooked	1 cup (250 mL)	40
Salmon, canned with bones	106.5 g (½ can)	225 to 243
Sardines, canned with bones	6 medium (72 g)	275
White beans, cooked	1 cup (250 mL)	170
Yogurt, plain	¾ cup (175 mL)	296

*Source: Calcium for Life and How Much Calcium Do We Need? Osteoporosis Society of Canada

Buying and Storing Almond Flour

Almond flour is available at many local health- and bulk-food stores, or in the bulk section of some grocery stores. When picking out your flour, make sure it's a light cream colour or a couple of shades lighter than butter. If it is oily, dark yellow, tan, or brown, it's rancid. Be particularly careful if you're buying flour from a retailer who stores it unrefrigerated or in direct sunlight.

Keep your almond flour cool, dry, and out of direct sunlight. We recommend refrigerating or freezing it. Almond flour will stay fresh for up to several weeks if refrigerated, and even longer if sealed in an air-tight package. If you freeze your flour, it can last for months. Don't store almond flour with items that are pungent, such as onions, garlic, or fish, because almonds absorb odours easily.

Baking with Almond Flour

Almond flour behaves differently than grain flour. Grains are sticky, light, and starchy, whereas almond flour is heavier and coarser. Baked goods made with almond flour won't rise as high as those made with wheat flour—they may even sink slightly after coming out of the oven. It's also impossible to make pasta with almond flour, and making crispy cookies requires extra baking time.

However, almond flour is easier to work with in most types of recipes (pages 129–30). Every almond flour bread is a "quick bread"—no time needed for resting and rising, and no extra ingredients, such as baking powder and yeast.

Ordering Almond Flour

If you can't find almond flour in your area, you can order it from elsewhere in bulk.

In Canada:
J. Gourmet
http://www.jgourmet.ca
416.782.0045

In the United States:
Lucy's Kitchen Shop
http://www.lucyskitchenshop.com
Toll-free in the US 1.888.484.2126
Outside the US 360.647.2279

Honey—A Sweet Sensation

Honey is most likely the world's oldest known sweetener, having been used since the Stone Age. The benefits of using honey instead of refined sugar are similar to those of cooking with almond flour instead of grain flour.

- **Honey can be easier to digest.** Researchers aren't sure why, but many people with sensitive intestines tolerate honey better than refined sugar. A 2004 physician-run survey of patients with inflammatory bowel disease found that the Specific Carbohydrate Diet, which uses honey as a refined-sugar substitute, helped 84% of participants achieve remission—61% of the patients were off all medications. One of the reasons for this could be honey's shorter-chained sugars, which are broken down more easily by the digestive system.

- **Honey may help your heart.** A large study called the Nurses' Health Study found that women who eat a lot of refined sugars are more at risk for developing coronary heart disease; honey is a great alternative to refined sugar. Other study results show that honey increases blood anti-oxidants, which lower LDL (the "bad" cholesterol) and help to prevent blocked arteries that can cause angina, heart attack, and stroke.

- **Honey is nutritious.** Honey has trace amounts of vitamins and minerals, making it more nutritious than refined sugar (see chart below).

Nutritional Content for 1 Tbsp (21 g) Honey* Total calories: 64	
Nutrient	**Average Amount**
Water	3.6 g
Total Carbohydrates	17.46 g
Fructose	8.16 g
Glucose	6.57 g
Maltose	1.53 g
Sucrose	0.32 g
Other carbohydrates	0.85 g
Protein	0.06 g
Dietary Fibre	0.04 g
Vitamins and Minerals	
Folate	0.42 mcg
Continued on next page	

Nutritional Content for 1 Tbsp (21 g) Honey* (continued)	
Nutrient	**Average Amount**
Niacin	0.03 mg
Pantothenic Acid	0.01 mg
Riboflavin	0.01 mg
Thiamin	<0.002 mg
Vitamin B_6	0.01 mg
Vitamin C	0.11 mg
Calcium	1.27 mg
Copper	0.01 mg
Iron	0.09 mg
Magnesium	0.42 mg
Manganese	0.03 mg
Phosphorus	1.0 mg
Potassium	11.02 mg
Selenium	0.17 mg
Sodium	0.85 mg
Zinc	0.05 mg

*Source: Honey-Health and Therapuetic Qualities: "I'm Here to Tell You the Bear Facts About Honey." The National Honey Board.

Honey Fun Facts

Honey has antibiotic properties that kill the bacteria responsible for infections such as meningitis, pneumonia, and sinusitis. When applied to skin, it can even help to heal wounds, such as burns, amputations, cuts, bed sores, and skin ulcers. Research has also found that when athletes use honey as a carbohydrate source during exercise, their power and performance significantly improve.

Buying and Storing Honey

If you want your honey to have a slightly longer shelf life, buy pasteurized honey. Typically, pasteurization involves heating foods to specific temperatures for several minutes to kill harmful bacteria. However, the pasteurization temperature used for honey doesn't kill the spores of botulism-producing bacteria, which is why it's recommended that children under 12 months old shouldn't eat honey. Pasteurizing honey only destroys sugar-tolerant yeasts that can cause granulation (also known as crystallization) and fermentation.

Be aware that honey is sometimes mixed with other sweeteners. You should buy only honey labelled "pure honey." Honey also varies widely in terms of flavour. The honey produced by big manufacturers is a blend of different kinds of honey, so it always tastes the same—and is probably what most people expect honey to taste like. However, honey can taste quite different, depending on the plant from which the bees collect nectar. You might want to try different kinds of honey to see which ones you like best. All of our recipes were developed using blended honey from large manufacturers.

Store honey at room temperature or cooler. If honey is exposed to air, heat, and moisture for a prolonged period of time, it will darken, crystallize, and lose flavour and aroma. If it does crystallize, heat it gently on the stove or in the microwave until it liquefies, and use it as you would normally.

Cooking with Honey

Honey adds a rich taste and texture to foods that granulated sugar doesn't. But because honey is heavy and a liquid, it sometimes can't be used exactly like sugar. It's part of the reason most of the baked goods in this cookbook are soft and chewy rather than hard and crispy.

Honey Quick Tips

- Honey tends to stick to measuring cups and spoons, but if you coat them with a small drop of oil or water the honey will slide out more easily.

- Heat honey before adding it to a recipe and it will be easier to mix in with other ingredients.

- If you want to replace refined sugar with honey in your favourite recipes, remember that honey is, cup for cup, about twice as sweet. So use half as much honey as you would sugar. This is because honey contains the very sweet monosaccharide fructose.

Yogurt, Cheese, and Butter—Virtually Lactose-Free

Yogurt

Although store-bought yogurt that contains only milk ingredients and active bacterial culture is an adequate substitute for homemade yogurt, it still has too much lactose for some people to digest. When you make yogurt at home, you can control the amount of lactose in it by adjusting the length of time it ferments. The bacterial cultures that turn milk into yogurt consume the lactose during fermentation and leave a product that's easily digestible by most lactose-sensitive people. Store-bought yogurt is only fermented for a few hours, but we ferment our yogurt for 24 to 30 hours. The result is delicious, virtually lactose-free yogurt (see page 38 for the recipe for homemade yogurt).

For milk-based yogurt, we recommend using milk that contains only milk ingredients and added vitamins. When making yogurt from 10% (half-and-half), 18% (table), or 35% (whipping) cream, organic cream is a must. All other creams have additives and preservatives that you don't want in your yogurt. Organic milk is also guaranteed to be preservative-free.

To turn milk or cream into yogurt, a bacterial starter is required. You have a choice of two starters: plain yogurt that contains only milk ingredients with active bacterial culture, or powdered starter available at health-food stores.

Amazing Yogurt

Aside from tasting great, yogurt is another significant source of calcium (see chart page 18). Research has also shown that the bacteria in yogurt may help to prevent and fight diseases, such as cancer, and can keep diarrhea-causing intestinal bacteria at bay.

Cheese

Many cheeses are naturally almost lactose-free. That's because they ferment for long periods of time. As with yogurt, the bacterial cultures that turn milk into cheese consume the lactose during fermentation and leave a product that's easily digestible by most lactose-sensitive people. If you still get sick after eating these cheeses, you are probably reacting to the type of bacterial culture used, or you have a milk protein allergy.

Here's a list of virtually lactose-free cheeses

Asiago

Blue

Brick

Brie

Camembert

Cheddar
  (mild, medium,
  old and extra old*)

Colby

Edam

Gorgonzola

Gouda

Gruyère

Havarti

Jarlsberg

Limburger

Monterey (Jack)

Muenster

Parmesan

Port du Salut

Provolone

Roquefort

Romano

Stilton

Swiss

Uncreamed cottage cheese
  (dry curd)

* Note that some people may react to the bacterial culture used to make extra old cheddar cheese.

Butter

Although butter contains very little lactose (it's mostly fat), it's possible to further reduce the amount of lactose through a process called clarification. Clarified butter, sometimes called ghee, can be bought at some health food stores or prepared as follows.

1. Heat butter in a saucepan until it melts and light-coloured milk solids float to the top.

2. Remove the milk solids by scooping them out with a spoon.

3. Pour the remaining butter through a sieve into a heat-resistant jar. Store in the fridge as you would normal butter.

Eggs—Vitamin Power

If we asked you to identify one food that causes high cholesterol, your answer might be eggs, right? Wrong. The myth that eggs are a major contributor to heart disease and high blood cholesterol has been perpetuated for years, despite a large body of evidence that proves otherwise. For example, one study conducted by the Department of Nutrition at the Harvard School of Public Health showed that eating eggs doesn't increase the risk of heart disease in healthy adults.

How is this possible? Eggs are extremely high in cholesterol, and cholesterol contributes to heart disease. In fact, one large egg contains 71% of the amount of cholesterol you're supposed to eat in a day. But your body doesn't absorb most of the cholesterol you get from food. What you eat accounts for a mere 20% of the cholesterol in your body. It's actually your liver that produces most of your blood cholesterol—about 80%. And when you eat high-cholesterol foods, your liver compensates by producing less cholesterol.

So eating foods with cholesterol in them will only raise your blood cholesterol a bit. Some people are more sensitive to cholesterol in food than others, but, generally speaking, it's primarily the type and amount of fat in food—not cholesterol—that affect blood cholesterol levels. Not only that, but cholesterol isn't all bad. It's a basic part of our cells that is responsible for helping with digestion, producing hormones, and producing vitamin D.

When to Eat Fewer Eggs

You need to be more careful about the number of eggs you eat if you're diabetic, have high blood cholesterol levels, or if you eat a lot of other foods high in cholesterol and saturated fat.

Although eggs contain saturated fat, which increases blood cholesterol, and still must be eaten in moderation, they are not nearly as bad for you as they've been made out to be. A large egg only has 8% of the saturated fat you can eat in a day and has no hydrogenated fat; more than half of the fat in eggs is unsaturated (i.e., the "good" fat). Eggs also provide lots of important nutrients, such as iron, protein, riboflavin, folate, phosphorus, and vitamins A, D, E, B_{12} and B_6. Eating one egg a day is considered to be not only safe but also healthy for many people.

How to Store Your Food

For many people, storing food in the refrigerator is a guessing game—they wait until leftovers look like a science experiment and then throw them away. Here are some guidelines for storing foods from our recipes safely. Follow these guidelines unless otherwise directed in the recipe. Always refrigerate or freeze leftovers within 2 hours of cooking.

Food Item	In the Refrigerator 4°C (40°F) or colder	In the Freezer −18°C (0°F) or colder
Beef, Poultry, and Fish		
Casseroles	1 to 2 days	2 to 3 months
Chicken, turkey, or beef burgers	1 to 2 days	1 to 3 months
Cooked fish and seafood	1 to 2 days	1 to 3 months
Cooked meat and meat dishes (e.g., stew, baked chicken, meatloaf)	3 to 4 days	2 to 3 months
Gravy and meat broth (chicken or fish soup/stock)	1 to 2 days	2 to 3 months
Leftover meat dishes with sauce	1 to 2 days	6 months
Dairy Products		
Butter	1 to 2 weeks	6 to 9 months
Hard cheeses	6 months unopened, 3 to 4 weeks opened	6 months
Milk	5 days past carton date	1 month (freezing affects flavour and appearance)

Continued on next page

Food Item	In the Refrigerator 4°C (40°F) or colder	In the Freezer –18°C (0°F) or colder
Yogurt	10 days	
Yogurt cheese/cream cheese	10 days	
Frozen yogurt		2 to 3 months
Eggs		
Fresh, in shell	3 to 5 weeks	
Hard-boiled	1 week	
Liquid pasteurized eggs, opened	3 days	1 year
Liquid pasteurized eggs, unopened	10 days	1 year
Omelettes	2 to 3 days	
Raw yolks, whites	2 to 4 days	1 year separated yolks and whites, 6 months beaten whole egg
Scrambled	1 to 2 days	
Egg-Containing		
Cheese Blintzes	2 to 3 days	2 to 3 months
Homemade mayonnaise	2 to 3 weeks	
Non-dairy ice cream		1 month
Quiche	2 to 3 days	
Soufflé bread	1 week	2 months

Continued on next page

Food Item	At Room Temperature	In the Refrigerator 4°C (40°F) or colder	In the Freezer −18°C (0°F) or colder
Almond-Flour Baked Goods			
Cookies (crispy) in an airtight container	2 months		3 months
Cookies (soft)	1 week	2 weeks	2 to 3 months
Crackers in an airtight container	2 months		3 months
Muffins, cakes, pizza, and breads	2 days	1 week	2 to 3 months
Pies	1 to 2 days	4 days	2 to 3 months
Appetizers and side dishes		2 to 4 days	2 to 3 months
Candy		1 to 2 weeks	2 to 3 months
Sauces, dips, soups, and chilis		1 to 2 days	2 to 3 months

Substitutions

People who are on the Specific Carbohydrate Diet (SCD), or suffer from Crohn's disease, ulcerative colitis, celiac disease, irritable bowel syndrome, autism, or a generally sensitive digestive system, often find that they react to small amounts of sugar, starch, or lactose found in commercial products. Therefore, we have simplified the way we list ingredients in our recipes to accommodate both the general public and SCDers. **Ingredients marked with an asterisk (*) can be replaced with either SCD-friendly or mainstream alternatives, depending on your need, and are listed in the substitution chart below.**

Convenience Foods That...	Substitutions for Sensitive Stomachs
May contain added sugars	
14 oz (398 mL) canned whole tomatoes with their juice	9 oz (250 g) peeled plum tomatoes and ½ cup (125 mL) tomato juice
19 oz (540 mL) canned whole tomatoes with their juice	12 oz (375 g) peeled plum tomatoes and 1 cup (250 mL) tomato juice
28 oz (796 ml) canned whole tomatoes with their juice	1 lb (500 g) peeled plum tomatoes and 1¼ cup (300 mL) tomato juice
48 oz (1.36 L) canned whole tomatoes with their juice	1¾ lb (875 g) peeled plum tomatoes and 2¼ cups (550 mL) tomato juice
Canned crushed tomatoes	Equivalent weight in canned tomato juice
Canned tomato paste	Homemade tomato paste (page 42)
Commercial tomato sauce	Homemade tomato sauce (page 41)

Continued on next page

Convenience Foods That...	Substitutions for Sensitive Stomachs
May contain added sugars	
Commercial fruit-sweetened jam	Homemade Strawberry Jam (page 189)
Commercial mayonnaise	Homemade Mayonnaise (page 47)
Commercial unsweetened applesauce	Homemade Applesauce (page 146)
Prepared chicken soup/stock	Homemade Chicken Soup (page 68)
Rice vinegar	Apple cider vinegar
May contain hidden starches or thickeners	
Commercial fruit-sweetened jam	Homemade Strawberry Jam (page 189)
Commercial sausage	Homemade Chicken Sausage Patties (page 103) or store-bought sausage without fillers or sugar
Ginger powder	Freshly grated ginger

Continued on next page

Convenience Foods That...	Substitutions for Sensitive Stomachs
Contain lactose	
Commercial yogurt	Homemade Yogurt (page 38)
Organic 10% (half-and-half) cream	Homemade Yogurt made with 10% (half-and-half) organic cream (page 38)
Organic 18% cream	Homemade Yogurt made with 18% organic cream (page 38)
Organic whipping cream	Homemade Yogurt made with organic whipping cream (page 38)
Organic cream cheese	Homemade Cream Cheese (page 40) or Yogurt Cheese (page 39)

BEGINNINGS AND SIDES

Sauces, Dips, and Dressings • Appetizers and Salads • Soups and Side Dishes

Many store-bought sauces, dressings, and dips are loaded with refined sugar, lactose, and starches. But it's possible to make these same foods without fillers and ingredients that are hard to digest. Believe it or not, you don't need starch to make a sauce thick, and you don't need sugar to make a salad dressing flavourful.

Even our appetizers, conveniently bite-sized, use everything from vegetables to eggs to hold their tasty fillings. Finger food, amuse-bouche, hors d'oeuvres. Whatever you call them—those pieces of heaven, which often involve pastry, are a true luxury. Fortunately, you don't have to ditch entertaining (or indulgent snacking) just because you don't eat grains.

The salads, soups, and side dishes in this section use common ingredients, sometimes in new ways, to give you grain-free and refined-sugar-free options that round out your meals. It might seem impossible to create hearty soups without thickening agents such as potatoes, starches, wheat flour, or prepackaged seasonings. But with the right techniques, herbs, and spices, you'll never miss your old recipes.

Sauces, Dips, and Dressings

Yogurt

Makes 8 cups (2 L)

Whether you make yogurt with milk or cream, the process is the same. The only difference is the consistency of the final product. Cream produces a thicker yogurt with more fat compared to yogurt made from milk. If you have any digestive issues, we suggest you use nothing with less fat than homogenized milk for homemade yogurt. Whatever yogurt you choose to make, you can eat it plain, sweetened with a bit of honey, or piled high with fresh fruit. Don't use your homemade yogurt as a starter for the next batch or the fermentation will be less effective.

8 cups (2 L) **pasteurized, organic milk** or **cream**

½ cup (125 mL) **plain, store-bought yogurt** or **2 packages powdered yogurt starter**

1. Bring the milk or cream to a boil and immediately remove it from the stove.

2. Cool to room temperature or cooler. You can refrigerate it to speed up the process.

3. If you're using plain yogurt as a starter, pour 1 cup (250 mL) of the milk or cream into a separate bowl, add the yogurt, and mix well. If you're using powdered yogurt starter, pour 2 packages (10 g) of starter into a bowl and add 1 cup (250 mL) of milk or cream. Mix well.

4. Add the starter mixture to the rest of the milk or cream and combine well.

5. Pour into a yogurt maker and follow the manufacturer's instructions, **but not the suggested fermentation time**.

6. Plug in the yogurt maker and **let the yogurt ferment for 24 to 30 hours**. Most people find that 24 hours is enough.

7. After 24 to 30 hours, refrigerate the yogurt for 6 to 8 hours to allow it to firm up and thicken.

Yogurt Cheese

Makes 1½ to 2 cups (375 to 500 mL)

Yogurt cheese is simple to make, versatile, and a great substitute for whipping cream with the addition of a little honey and vanilla.

1. Soak the cotton bag that comes with your yogurt maker in boiling water for about 1 minute. Spoon the yogurt into the bag and hang it on a cupboard handle or nail. The yogurt will start dripping as soon as it's in the bag, so make sure there's a container under it.

2. Alternatively, you can drip yogurt in a colander or sieve lined with cheesecloth.

3. Let drip until it thickens to your liking, about 6 to 8 hours. Store in the refrigerator.

4 cups (1 L) **homemade Yogurt** (page 38) or **plain store-bought yogurt**

Cream Cheese

Serves 4 to 6

There are few foods more decadent than cream cheese. It's easy to make your own low-lactose cream cheese once you've made a batch of Yogurt Cheese. Cream cheese is perfect with crackers (pages 136, 141, 142), bread (pages 132–34) or vegetables.

2 cups (500 mL) **Yogurt Cheese** (page 39)

¼ tsp (1 mL) **salt** or to taste

1. Scoop the dripped yogurt into a container and mix in the salt. Taste and add more salt if you feel it's necessary.

Tomato Sauce

Makes 3 cups (750 mL)

This recipe is simple and adaptable. If you're not a fan of oregano, use more basil. If you prefer less garlic, use less of it. Don't be afraid to experiment! Use this sauce with Spaghetti Squash (page 78) or Meatloaf (page 101).

1. Put all the ingredients except for the honey in a medium-sized pot.

2. Simmer uncovered over medium heat for about 1 ½ hours, or until it has thickened to your liking.

3. Add the honey and mix well.

4. Let cool, discard the bay leaves, and store in a jar in the refrigerator or freezer.

3 large **garlic cloves**, pressed

1 **small onion**, diced

2 tsp (10 mL) **dried basil**

2 tsp (10 mL) **dried oregano**

2 **bay leaves**

½ tsp (2 mL) **dried thyme**

½ tsp (2 mL) **salt**

¼ tsp (1 mL) **black pepper**

One 48-oz (1.3-L) can **tomato juice**

1 Tbsp (15 mL) **honey**

Tomato Paste

Makes 1 cup (250 mL)

Homemade tomato paste, although not as thick as commercial tomato paste, is easy to make and has a more delicate taste than the canned variety. Be sure you are making your paste from tomato juice that has no added salt or sugar. This paste is great as a sauce for Gourmet Pizza (page 144) or when making Sweet and Sour Barbecue Sauce (page opposite).

One 48-oz (1.3-L) can **tomato juice**

1. Pour the tomato juice into a medium-sized pot over medium heat.

2. Bring to a boil, watching that it doesn't boil over.

3. Reduce the heat to low. Continue to simmer uncovered, or with a mesh cover or strainer over the opening of the pot to minimize the splatter. You want the moisture in the juice to evaporate, so don't completely cover the pot with a lid.

4. Stir occasionally, reducing the heat as the sauce gets thicker, and continue to cook for approximately 1 ¼ hours until it is reduced to 1 cup (250 mL).

5. Refrigerate for up to 2 weeks or freeze.

Sweet and Sour Barbecue Sauce

Makes 1¼ cups (300 mL)

Commercial barbecue sauces are saturated with sugar and syrups, and thickened with starches and gums. This sauce is pure and simple to make. It's delicious on Sweet and Sour Chicken Wings (page 110) or ribs. Eliminate the optional spices if you're sensitive to them.

1. Place all the ingredients in a small saucepan over medium heat and stir until combined.

2. Bring to a boil and let boil for 5 minutes. Remove from the heat.

3. Use immediately or cool and store in the refrigerator.

⅔ cup (150 mL) **Tomato Paste**＊

⅔ cup (150 mL) **white vinegar**

½ cup (125 mL) **honey**

2 **garlic cloves**, pressed (optional)

¼ tsp (1 mL) **paprika** or **cayenne pepper** (optional)

½ tsp (2 mL) **red pepper flakes** (optional)

Salt and **black pepper** to taste

＊ See pages 31 to 33 for the substitution chart that lists convenience foods and SCD alternatives.

Cocktail Sauce

Makes almost ½ cup (125 mL)

Cocktail sauce is the quintessential dipping sauce for shrimp or other seafood, but the original is loaded with sugar and starches. This version is every bit as good as the bottled stuff!

¼ cup (50 mL) **Tomato Paste**∗

2 Tbsp (25 mL) **bottled white horseradish** containing only horseradish, vinegar, and salt

2 tsp (10 mL) **honey**

½ tsp (2 mL) **lemon juice**

∗ See pages 31 to 33 for the substitution chart that lists convenience foods and SCD alternatives.

1. Mix all ingredients in a bowl and refrigerate until serving time.

Baba Ganouj

Serves 4 to 6

Jenny has known Paul since she was four years old. When she was little, he was her best friend's "icky older brother." When they grew up, Jenny learned to appreciate Paul's many talents, one of which is making the world's best baba ganouj, from a recipe passed on to him from his mother, Liz. Enjoy Paul and Liz's dip with vegetables, bread (pages 132–34) or crackers (page 136, 141, 142).

1. Holding the eggplant with tongs, cook directly on your stove burner (gas or electric) or on a barbecue. Rotate it as it cooks until it is evenly very soft, smoking, and blackened.

2. Place the cooked eggplant in a bowl of cool water and remove the skin.

3. Lightly oil a small frying pan and brown the garlic lightly over low heat.

4. Put the garlic, salt, pepper, paprika, oil, lemon juice, and soft, skinless eggplant in a blender and purée until smooth.

1 **eggplant**

2 **garlic cloves**, coarsely diced

Salt, black pepper, and **paprika** to taste

2 Tbsp (25 mL) **olive oil**

2 tsp (10 mL) **lemon juice**

Tzatziki

Makes about 2 cups (500 mL)

This wonderful dip is best when made with homemade 10% organic cream yogurt (page 38). Lower-fat yogurts can also be used—they simply require more dripping time, and may result in a thinner, tarter dip. Add all the ingredients before dripping the yogurt to allow the flavours to combine. This dip is best made the day before and dripped overnight.

1 **large cucumber**

½ Tbsp (7.5 mL) pressed **garlic**

½ Tbsp (7.5 mL) **white vinegar**

¼ tsp (1 mL) **olive oil**

2 cups (500 mL) **Yogurt***

Salt and **black pepper** to taste

* See pages 31 to 33 for the substitution chart that lists convenience foods and SCD alternatives.

1. Peel the cucumber and cut it in half lengthwise. Remove the seeds and discard. Coarsely grate the cucumber by hand or with a food processor.

2. Put the grated cucumber in a dish towel and twist it to squeeze out the excess liquid.

3. Add the cucumber, garlic, vinegar, and oil to the yogurt.

4. Place the yogurt in a colander lined with a cheesecloth or coffee filter, or use a yogurt cheese maker. Let it drip overnight or until it reaches a consistency you like.

5. Add salt and pepper before serving.

Mayonnaise

Makes 1 ¼ cups (300 mL)

Nothing tastes better than homemade mayonnaise. Along with a lighter and fresher taste, there are the benefits of no preservatives or sugar. Refrigerate for up to 3 weeks.

1. Place the egg, vinegar or juice, mustard, salt, pepper, and optional honey in the food processor or blender.

2. With the machine running on high, **slowly** drizzle in the oil.

3. If you prefer a thicker mayonnaise, add more oil.

1 **whole egg**

1 tsp (5 mL) **white vinegar** or fresh **lemon juice**

1 tsp (5 mL) **Dijon mustard**

Pinch **kosher salt**

Pinch **black pepper**

Tiny dribble of **honey** (optional)

1 cup (250 mL) **sunflower oil**

Making Perfect Mayo

The most common complaint about homemade mayonnaise is that the ingredients separate. This happens when you don't add the oil slowly enough to properly emulsify the mixture. The second-biggest complaint is that oil dribbles all over the food processor or blender while it's added in a slow stream. Here is an easy tip that takes care of both these problems. Purchase a plastic squeeze bottle similar to the kind ketchup is served in at a delicatessen. Pour the oil into the squeeze bottle and turn it upside down with the spout sitting in the feeding hole or tube. With the motor running, use firm pressure to slowly squeeze the oil out of the bottle. Count to 60 in your head while drizzling. If you still have oil left in the bottle after 60 seconds, you're going slowly enough and will achieve the proper emulsification.

Honey-Dijon Vinaigrette

Makes ¾ cup (175 mL)

This salad dressing is sweet and refreshing. It's perfect on a salad made savoury by grilled chicken, salmon, or Parmesan cheese. Refrigerate for up to 3 weeks.

¼ cup (50 mL) **olive oil**

¼ cup (50 mL) unsweetened **rice vinegar***

1 tsp (5 mL) **sesame oil**

1 ½ Tbsp (22.5 mL) **honey**

2 Tbsp (25 mL) **Dijon mustard**

1 tsp (5 mL) freshly grated **ginger**

---

*See pages 31 to 33 for the substitution chart that lists convenience foods and SCD alternatives.

1. In a bowl, combine the olive oil, vinegar, sesame oil, and honey.

2. Add the mustard and whisk to emulsify.

3. Add the grated ginger.

4. Use immediately or refrigerate. Bring to room temperature before serving.

Go Asian

Freshly grated ginger adds a tang and Asian flavour to any dish. Fresh ginger is easy to peel and grate: use the tip of a small spoon to peel the skin off the ginger, and then grate it coarsely or finely with a hand grater. Freeze your leftover fresh ginger. It's easy to grate and the flavour will be almost as good as fresh.

Spiced Honey Chicken

**Salade Niçoise
with Fresh Tuna**

Basil-Cider Vinaigrette

Makes ¾ cup (175 mL)

This salad dressing is delicious on a more hearty lettuce, such as romaine, and is perfectly paired with Sunflower Salad (page 65). The basil and garlic are a great combination. However, you can reduce or omit the garlic if you're sensitive to it.

1. Combine all the ingredients in a jar and shake well. The mustard emulsifies the oil and vinegar and stops them from separating.

2. Store in the refrigerator for up to 3 weeks. Bring to room temperature before serving.

¼ cup (50 mL) **apple cider vinegar**

¼ cup (50 mL) **olive oil**

2 Tbsp (25 mL) **water**

1 Tbsp (15 mL) **Dijon mustard**

1 **garlic clove**, pressed

2 Tbsp (25 mL) chopped **fresh basil**

Salt and **black pepper** to taste

Refrigerating Olive Oil

Bring dressings containing olive oil to room temperature before serving. Olive oil tends to congeal when refrigerated.

Salmon Mousse

Makes one 8- x 4-inch (1.5-L) loaf

This salmon mousse is the perfect appetizer for a crowd, and is best if made a day ahead. Using canned salmon makes this dish easy to pull together. Serve it with crackers (pages 136, 141, 142) or vegetables.

¼ cup (50 mL) **cold water**

1 Tbsp (15 mL) or 1 package **gelatin**

½ cup (125 mL) **boiling water**

One 7 ½ -oz (213-mL) can **salmon**, drained

½ cup (125 mL) **dry-curd cottage cheese** (see page opposite) or **Cream Cheese***

1 Tbsp (15 mL) **water**

1 Tbsp (15 mL) **lemon juice**

Dash **hot pepper sauce**

¼ tsp (1 mL) **paprika**

½ tsp (2 mL) **salt**

Pinch freshly ground **black pepper**

2 Tbsp (25 mL) finely chopped **fresh dill**

1 **egg white**

Pinch **salt**

½ cup (125 mL) **whipping cream Yogurt***

* See pages 31 to 33 for the substitution chart that lists convenience foods and SCD alternatives.

1. Pour the cold water in a small bowl and sprinkle the gelatin over it. Allow the gelatin to dissolve.

2. Add the boiling water and stir until the gelatin is melted.

3. In the food processor or blender, mix the salmon and dry-curd cottage cheese or Yogurt Cheese, 1 Tbsp (15 mL) of the water, and the lemon juice. Blend until you have a smooth mixture, scraping down the sides as necessary.

4. Add the hot pepper sauce, paprika, salt, pepper, and dill. Blend again.

5. Add the dissolved gelatin and blend once more. Adding the gelatin will make the mixture smooth and more liquid.

6. Pour the mixture into a glass or metal bowl and refrigerate it.

7. Line the bottom of a loaf pan or mould with a piece of parchment paper.

8. Beat the egg white with a pinch of salt until stiff but not dry. Set aside.

9. Beat the whipping cream yogurt into soft peaks. Do not overbeat.

10. Remove the salmon mixture from the fridge. It should be cold and just beginning to set around the edges.

11. Gently fold the beaten egg white into the salmon mixture. It may be a little difficult to fold, but try not to stir all the air out of the mixture.

12. Fold the whipped yogurt into the mixture.

13. Spoon the mixture into the loaf pan or mould. Cover the top of the mixture with another piece of parchment paper, and refrigerate for at least 6 hours until it has set.

14. When it's set, remove the top piece of parchment. Carefully run a hot, wet knife around the edges of the loaf pan or mould to release the mousse from the sides. Place a decorative serving plate over the top and invert it. Slowly lift away the loaf pan or mould and peel off the parchment paper. Garnish with a sprig or two of dill.

Dry-Curd Cottage Cheese

Dry-curd cottage cheese is also known as farmer cheese, bakers' cheese, or pressed dry cottage cheese. This cheese is a white, dry curd that hasn't had fluid added to it after fermentation. Dry-curd cottage cheese is treated with a bacterial culture that reduces residual lactose. In many recipes, it's a good substitute for Yogurt or Yogurt Cheese—simply add water to moisten it.

Caesar Salad Dressing

Makes 2 cups (500 mL)

This garlicky dressing is creamy but not thick, and light but full of flavour. Use freshly grated Italian Parmesan cheese—the canned cheese found on supermarket shelves is processed with fillers and preservatives so that it no longer requires refrigeration. You can substitute red wine vinegar for the white; it will just give the dressing a slightly pink hue. This is easier to make if you use a food processor or blender.

1 coddled **egg**

½ cup (125 mL) **white wine vinegar**

2 Tbsp (25 mL) **lemon juice**

2 **garlic cloves**

½ tsp (2 mL) **salt**

¼ tsp (1 mL) freshly ground **black pepper**

¾ cup (175 mL) **olive oil**

⅓ cup (75 mL) freshly grated **Parmesan cheese**

1. In a blender or the work bowl of your food processor, place the coddled egg (scraping the sides of the shell to get out all the egg), vinegar, lemon juice, garlic, salt, and pepper. Blend until well mixed.

2. While the processor or blender is running, gradually drizzle in the oil.

3. Add the Parmesan cheese and pulse a few times to mix.

4. Use immediately or refrigerate for up to 1 week. This dressing will thicken in the fridge. Bring to room temperature before serving.

Coddled Eggs

To coddle an egg, cook it briefly in its shell in boiling water. Bring water to a boil in a small pot. Carefully lower the egg into the boiling water for 60 seconds. At the 60-second mark, remove the egg and run it under cold water to stop the cooking process.

Appetizers and Salads

Parmesan-stuffed Mushroom Caps

Serves 4 as an appetizer

After trying these delicious little appetizers, you'll wonder why they're traditionally stuffed with bread crumbs. The sharp, tangy taste of freshly grated Parmesan cheese is a far better choice.

16 medium brown **mushroom caps**

3 **green onions**, finely chopped

1 **garlic clove**, pressed

½ cup (125 mL) plus 2 Tbsp (25 mL) grated **Parmesan cheese**

2 Tbsp (25 mL) **Mayonnaise***

Salt and **black pepper** to taste

* See pages 31 to 33 for the substitution chart that lists convenience foods and SCD alternatives.

1. Heat the oven to 350°F (180°C).

2. Brush the mushrooms clean with a paper towel. Do not wash mushrooms in water.

3. Separate the stems from the caps, and set the stems aside. If necessary, hollow out the caps a bit with a knife to allow for more filling space.

4. Finely chop the mushroom stems.

5. Mix together the chopped stems, onions, garlic, ½ cup (125 mL) Parmesan cheese, mayonnaise, salt, and pepper.

6. Place each mushroom cap open-side up in a small casserole dish. A mini muffin tin can also be used to hold the mushrooms, which will allow the moisture that accumulates during baking to pool in the space below each mushroom.

7. Mound the mixture into the caps and sprinkle the remaining Parmesan cheese over top.

8. Bake until melted and heated through, approximately 10 to 15 minutes.

Variation: Escargot Mushroom Caps

Go gourmet by stuffing each mushroom with an escargot and topping with the same mixture.

Marinated Asparagus Squares

Makes 25 pieces

This is a wonderfully flavourful hors d'oeuvre to pass around at a dinner party. Making part of this dish a day or two before cuts down on preparation time the day of the party. The recipe can be doubled to fill a 9- x 13-inch (3.5-L) casserole dish. In this case, double the baking time to 1 hour.

1. Chop the asparagus into 1-inch (2.5-cm) pieces (discard the woody bottom inch), and steam until just soft. Drain.

2. Place in a non-reactive bowl with the vinegar, salt, and pepper.

3. Let the asparagus pieces marinate overnight or for up to 2 days.

4. Preheat the oven to 350°F (180°C).

5. Heat the oil in a medium-sized saucepan and sauté the onion and garlic over low to medium heat until soft.

6. Add the marinated asparagus and cook for 1 minute to let the flavours combine.

7. Add the parsley, oregano, salt, and pepper. Let the mixture cool.

8. When the asparagus mixture is cool, add the eggs.

9. Combine the cheddar cheese and almond flour. Add to the asparagus mixture and combine well.

10. Spread evenly into an 8- x 8-inch (2-L) square pan and bake for 30 minutes.

11. Let rest for a few minutes before slicing into squares. Serve warm.

½ lb (250 g) **asparagus**

2 Tbsp (25 mL) **red wine vinegar**

Salt and **black pepper** to taste

1 Tbsp (15 mL) **olive oil**

1 **onion**, finely chopped

2 **garlic cloves**, pressed

½ cup (125 mL) finely chopped **fresh parsley**

½ tsp (2 mL) **dried oregano**

4 **eggs**, lightly beaten

½ lb (250 g) **cheddar cheese**, grated

½ cup (125 mL) **almond flour**

Thai Chicken Wraps

Makes 40 pieces

These Thai chicken wraps are great for a party. Prepare the marinade, crêpes, and dipping sauce a day ahead, then cook the chicken and roll the wraps the day of the party. The egg crêpe is just as delicious as the traditional rice-paper wrap.

Marinade

¾ lb (375 g) boneless, skinless **chicken thighs**

2 stalks **lemon grass**, sliced into thin 1½-inch (4-cm) long strips

3 Tbsp (45 mL) chopped **fresh basil**

2 large **garlic cloves**, pressed

2 Tbsp (25 mL) chopped **spring onion**

2 Tbsp (25 mL) very finely chopped **red bell pepper**

Pinch **red pepper flakes**

2 Tbsp (25 mL) **olive oil**

1 Tbsp (15 mL) **honey**

Juice of 1 **lemon**

Marinade

1. Place the chicken between sheets of waxed paper and pound with a mallet or heavy frying pan to ¼-inch (5-mm) thickness. Refrigerate.

2. Combine all the remaining ingredients in a medium-sized, non-reactive bowl.

3. Add the pounded chicken and toss to evenly coat.

4. Refrigerate for 6 hours or overnight.

Dipping Sauce

1. Combine all the ingredients in a small saucepan and bring to a boil.

2. Boil for 5 minutes.

3. Cool in the refrigerator.

Crêpes

1. Crack the eggs into a large bowl, and whisk together with the egg whites and water.

2. Grease an 8-inch (20-cm) non-stick omelette pan and bring to medium heat.

3. Pour 3 Tbsp (45 mL) of the egg mixture (use a ¼-cup/50-mL measure and fill it ¾ of the way full) into the pan, and swirl it around to evenly coat the bottom of the pan. Cook until the egg sets on top.

4. Flip the crêpe over and briefly cook on the second side.

5. When cooked, remove and stack on a plate.

6. Repeat steps 2 to 5 until all the egg is used up. You should have 8 crêpes. Refrigerate until ready to assemble.

Continued on next page

Dipping Sauce

3 Tbsp (45 mL) **white vinegar**

¼ cup (50 mL) **honey**

¼ cup (50 mL) **water**

2 drops **sesame oil**

Pinch **salt**

⅛ tsp (.5 mL) **garlic chili sauce** (no sugar added) or less, or ½ tsp (2 mL) pressed garlic and a pinch of red pepper flakes

Crêpes

3 extra-large **eggs**

½ cup (125 mL) **egg whites** (4 egg whites)

2 Tbsp (25 mL) **water**

Butter, oil, or **non-stick spray**

Thai Chicken Wraps (continued)

Assembly

Fresh chives for tying wraps

Assembly

1. Remove the chicken from the marinade and wipe it clean.

2. In a medium-sized frying pan with a bit of oil, cook each piece of chicken on high heat until browned and cooked through.

3. Remove from the frying pan and set aside until cool enough to handle. Slice the chicken into long, thin strips. Refrigerate or assemble immediately.

4. Using a 2-inch (5-cm) round cookie cutter, cut 5 circles from each crêpe.

5. Take one long chive and place it horizontally on a clean work surface.

6. Put a crêpe circle on top of the chive.

7. Lay 2 to 3 thin strips of chicken on top of the crêpe vertically. The chicken can extend beyond the crêpe.

8. Close the crêpe around the chicken by tying the chive into a knot. Cut off the excess chive.

9. Repeat with each crêpe circle.

10. Serve at room temperature with dipping sauce.

Cold Marinated Shrimp

Serves 4 to 6 as an appetizer

Often the simplest of recipes yields the most wonderful results. This is one of those dishes. A Bager family favourite, it's great to have in the fridge for a quick snack, part of a meal, or to fill out a meal of leftovers. Don't use big, fancy, expensive shrimp for this recipe—the frozen, precooked ones you find in a ring in your local grocery store are best.

1. Place all the ingredients in a flat-bottomed serving bowl.

2. Toss to coat each shrimp in sauce, cover, and marinate in the fridge for 6 to 12 hours. The longer it sits, the more flavourful it will become.

3. Serve cold from the fridge.

2 frozen cooked **shrimp rings**, defrosted

1 **red onion**, thinly sliced

1 **garlic clove**, pressed

½ cup (125 mL) **sunflower oil**

½ cup (125 mL) **white vinegar**

Salt and **black pepper** to taste

Coleslaw

Serves 10

This coleslaw is a variation of the best homemade coleslaw we've ever eaten—Judy Bager's. It's very garlicky, so you may choose to reduce the size or number of garlic cloves.

¾ head **green cabbage**

1 large **red bell pepper**

2 large **garlic cloves**, pressed

1 tsp (5 mL) **salt** or to taste

½ tsp (2 mL) **black pepper** or to taste

1 tsp (5 mL) **Dijon mustard**

½ cup (125 mL) **white vinegar**

¼ cup (50 mL) **olive oil**

1. Finely grate the cabbage and red pepper by hand or in the food processor. Transfer to a large bowl.

2. Add the garlic, salt, pepper, mustard, vinegar, and oil, and toss.

3. Refrigerate for a few hours to marinate and allow the flavours to intensify.

Variation: Classic Coleslaw

Substitute 2 large carrots for the red pepper, and add ½ tsp (2 mL) honey. All the other ingredients remain the same.

Sunflower Salad

Makes 6 appetizer portions

The sunflower seeds add crunch, eliminating the need for croutons and adding a whole new dimension to the salad. Turn this appetizer for six into a meal for two by adding canned or fresh salmon, or grilled chicken, before tossing with the dressing.

1. Combine all the salad ingredients and toss with half the dressing. Taste, and add more dressing if necessary.

2 **romaine hearts**, chopped

2 cups (500 mL) **baby spinach**

½ cup (125 mL) grated **Parmesan cheese**

¼ cup (50 mL) **sunflower seeds**

Basil-Cider Vinaigrette (page 53)

Salade Niçoise with Fresh Tuna

Serves 4 as a main dish

Salade niçoise typically calls for boiled white potatoes. Our version omits the potatoes and uses fresh tuna rather than canned, which makes this salad perfect for an elegant lunch or dinner. Since the tuna in this recipe is seared and not cooked through, ensure that you get your fish from a reputable fishmonger.

1 lb (500 g) fresh **tuna steak**

Olive oil for brushing

Freshly cracked **black pepper**

4 hard-boiled **eggs**

4 **tomatoes**

3 **romaine hearts**

Kosher salt

Basil-Cider Vinaigrette (page 53)

1. Brush the tuna with olive oil on both sides, sprinkle liberally with cracked black pepper, and refrigerate for 30 minutes.

2. Slice the eggs into rounds, dice the tomatoes, and wash and dry the lettuce. Set aside.

3. Heat a cast-iron pan on high.

4. Just before cooking, liberally salt the fish on both sides.

5. When the pan is smoking, sear the tuna for 2 minutes on each side.

6. Remove from the heat and let sit for 1 minute before slicing with the grain.

7. Add the tomatoes to the lettuce and toss with ¼ cup (50 mL) of the dressing or to taste. Divide among the plates.

8. Decorate each serving with egg rounds and top with the seared tuna.

Soups and Side Dishes

Chicken Soup
Serves 8 to 12

There's nothing quite as comforting as homemade chicken soup. Because this recipe is made with chicken bones, it's particularly economical, easy, and low in fat. The addition of tomato paste is the secret ingredient: it adds depth of flavour. Serve as is or use it to make Seafood Dumpling Soup (page opposite). You can also freeze smaller portions of the strained liquid for use as stock in other recipes.

16 cups (4 L) **water**

3 large **carrots**, cut into large chunks

5 stalks **celery**, cut into large chunks

2 medium **onions**, quartered

1 small bunch **fresh parsley**

2 lb (1 kg) **chicken bones**

2 Tbsp (25 mL) **Tomato Paste***
(optional)

Salt and **black pepper** to taste

*See pages 31 to 33 for the substitution chart that lists convenience foods and SCD alternatives.

1. Fill a large stockpot with cold water.

2. Add the carrots, celery, onions, parsley, and chicken bones.

3. Cover the pot and bring to a boil.

4. Reduce the heat to low, cover, and continue to cook for 2 hours.

5. Remove the solid ingredients from the soup and refrigerate.

6. Add the tomato paste to the pot.

7. Simmer **uncovered** for 3 hours.

8. Add salt and pepper to taste.

9. Cool to room temperature before refrigerating.

10. Once cold, a thin layer of fat will form on the top of the soup. This coagulated fat can easily be lifted off the soup and discarded.

11. Strain the soup.

12. Remove the chicken that was left on the bones. Add the chicken and vegetables back to the soup before reheating and serving.

Variation: Chicken Stock

If you want to use this soup as a chicken stock, simply omit step 12.

Seafood Dumpling Soup

Serves 4 as an appetizer, 2 as a meal

Unlike traditional dumplings, these have no outer dough. Beaten egg whites are added to the fish and seafood to create a dumpling that's light and fluffy. The flavourful water left from cooking the dumplings is combined with chicken stock to make a savoury soup. A drop of sesame oil just before serving gives it a rich Asian flavour.

1. In a blender or food processor, combine the fish, shrimp, and egg yolk. Purée until the mixture is thick and smooth.

2. Transfer to a large work bowl.

3. Add the jalapeño pepper, anchovy paste, green onions, black pepper, and salt. Mix well.

4. Beat the egg whites into stiff peaks.

5. Gently fold the egg whites into the seasoned purée. Heat the water to boiling in a large pot.

6. Wet your hands and form the mixture into small balls the size of walnuts. You should get 30 dumplings.

7. Drop the dumplings into the boiling water as you make them, and boil for 2 minutes after you've dropped in the last one.

8. Remove the dumplings with a slotted spoon and set aside.

9. Add the chicken stock to the water. Taste, and season with salt and pepper if necessary.

10. Add the cabbage to the soup. Return to a boil and cook for 1 minute.

11. Return the dumplings to the pot and heat through, approximately 1 minute. Do not overcook or the dumplings will be tough.

12. Serve hot in big bowls with a drop of sesame oil.

1 lb (500 g) **halibut** or **sole**

½ lb (250 g) **raw shrimp** (shelled and deveined)

3 **eggs**, separated

1 Tbsp (15 mL) chopped **jalapeño pepper**

1½ Tbsp (22 mL) **anchovy paste** without additives

¼ cup (50 mL) chopped **green onions**

½ tsp (2 mL) **black pepper**

¼ tsp (1 mL) **salt**

4 cups (1 L) **water**

4 cups (1 L) **Chicken Stock***

1 head **napa cabbage**, chopped

Sesame oil

---

*See pages 31 to 33 for the substitution chart that lists convenience foods and SCD alternatives.

Asparagus and Cauliflower Soup

Serves 4 to 6 as an appetizer

This soup is thick and chunky because only part of the cauliflower is puréed. Although the recipe calls for cream, it can be omitted.

1 Tbsp (15 mL) **olive oil**

2 **small onions**, thinly sliced

1 **garlic clove**, pressed

4 cups (1 L) **asparagus** cut into 1-inch (2.5-cm) pieces

4 cups (1 L) **Chicken Stock***

¼ cup (50 mL) **organic 10% (half-and-half) cream** treated with Lactaid® drops (see below right)

2 Tbsp (25 mL) **butter**

1 **head cauliflower**, separated into florets and steamed

Salt and **black pepper** to taste

* See pages 31 to 33 for the substitution chart that lists convenience foods and SCD alternatives.

1. Heat the oil in a large pot over medium heat. Add the onions, garlic, and asparagus and cook until soft.

2. Add the chicken stock and bring to a boil. Simmer for 15 to 20 minutes.

3. Add the cream and butter. Boil for 2 minutes and then remove from the heat.

4. Purée the mixture with a blender or food processor.

5. Pass the mixture through a fine sieve and discard the fibrous parts.

6. Return the strained soup to the processor or blender and add half the steamed cauliflower. Purée and return the soup to the pot. If using a hand blender, return the strained soup to the pot, add half the steamed cauliflower, and purée.

7. Add the remaining steamed cauliflower to the soup and heat through.

8. Season with salt and pepper.

Reducing Lactose

If you're lactose-sensitive, organic cream can be used in small amounts if treated with Lactaid® drops. You can find these drops at drugstores. Be sure to follow the instructions on the package carefully.

Sweet and Spicy Squash Soup

Serves 4 to 6

To crank up the spice in this dish, add cayenne pepper, hot pepper flakes, or more black pepper. To reduce the spice, eliminate the pepper. This soup reheats well, so feel free to store individual portions in the freezer. It's great with bread (pages 132–34), salad (pages 64–66), crackers (pages 136, 141, 142), or on its own as a snack.

1. Preheat the oven to 375°F (190°C).

2. Place the three squash halves cut-side down in a casserole dish.

3. Pour in enough water to cover the bottom of the dish.

4. Bake for 45 to 60 minutes or until the squash pieces feel a bit soft when you press down on them.

5. Remove the squash pieces from the oven. When cool enough to handle, remove and discard the seeds.

6. Scoop out the cooked squash and set aside.

7. In a large pot over medium heat, melt the butter with the oil. Add the onion and garlic, and cook for about 5 minutes until the onion is translucent.

8. Add the squash, salt, oregano, basil, pepper, cinnamon, and water, and simmer for 20 minutes on medium heat with the lid of the pot ajar. Stir occasionally.

9. Remove the lid from the pot and cook for 8 to 10 more minutes.

10. Add the honey and mix well.

11. Cool for 10 minutes.

12. Purée until smooth.

13. Reheat and serve.

1½ **butternut squash**, cut lengthwise

1 Tbsp (15 mL) **butter**

1 Tbsp (15 mL) **olive oil**

1 **small onion**, diced

6 **garlic cloves**

½ tsp (2 mL) **salt**

½ tsp (2 mL) **dried oregano**

½ tsp (2 mL) **dried basil**

½ tsp (2 mL) **black pepper**

¼ tsp (1 mL) **ground cinnamon**

4 cups (1 L) **water**

3 Tbsp (45 mL) **honey**

Tomato, Spinach, and Lentil Soup

Serves 6 to 8

This hearty soup is perfect for a winter's day. The wonderfully aromatic cumin and ajowan give it Middle Eastern and Indian flavours. Roasting the spices releases the flavour and adds to the character of this soup. Ajowan can be found at Indian markets or stores that sell spices in bulk.

10 cups (2.5 L) **cold water**

2 cups (500 mL) soaked and rinsed **lentils** (see page opposite, steps 1 to 5)

2 cups (500 mL) soaked and rinsed **split peas** (see page opposite, steps 1 to 5)

3 large **carrots**, finely diced

5 stalks **celery**, finely diced

3 **leeks**, white parts only, cleaned well and finely sliced

One 48-oz (1.3-L) can **tomato juice**

6 cups (1.5 L) **fresh baby spinach**

2 tsp (10 mL) **olive oil**

2 tsp (10 mL) **black mustard seed**

1 tsp (5 mL) **fennel seed**

1 tsp (5 mL) **cumin seed**

½ tsp (2 mL) **ajowan seed**

Salt and **black pepper** to taste

1. Place the water in a large pot and add the prepared lentils and split peas.

2. Bring to a gentle boil and cook uncovered for 1 hour.

3. After 1 hour, add the carrots, celery, and leeks.

4. Continue to boil until the legumes are soft and the vegetables are cooked. Add the tomato juice and spinach. Reduce to a simmer.

5. Heat the olive oil in a saucepan over medium heat. Add the black mustard, fennel, cumin, and ajowan, and cook until they become aromatic and the seeds begin to pop.

6. Stir the spice mixture into the soup.

7. Season with salt and pepper.

Beans and Legumes—Easier to Digest

Beans, split peas, lentils, and peanuts all belong to the legume family. To minimize the bloating, gas, or discomfort you sometimes get with eating prepared legumes, you can soak them. Legumes double in bulk when soaked.

1. Put dried legumes in a large bowl and cover with water. Make sure the water level is 4 inches (10 cm) above the legumes because they'll absorb the liquid, expand, and double in bulk.

2. Soak in a cool place for 8 to 10 hours or overnight in the refrigerator.

3. Drain and rinse in a colander with cool, fresh water.

4. Put the legumes in a pot, cover with water, and bring to a boil.

5. As soon as they come to a boil, they'll start to foam. Remove from the heat, drain, and rinse them again. **At this point, they can be added to soups for further cooking. To fully cook the beans and store for future use, follow steps 6 and 7.**

6. Put the beans back in your pot and cover them with fresh water again. Boil for 30 to 45 minutes, or until they're tender.

7. Drain and use immediately, or freeze in smaller portions for use in other recipes.

Chunky Cabbage and Bean Soup

Serves 4 to 6

This dish is hearty enough to stand alone as a meal. If you're very hungry, try it with crackers (pages 136, 141, 142) or bread (pages 132–34). It reheats well, so feel free to store individual portions of it in the freezer.

2 Tbsp (25 mL) **olive oil**

1 cup (250 mL) **diced onion**

⅔ cup (150 mL) **sliced carrot**

2 **garlic cloves**, finely diced

4 cups (1 L) fully cooked
navy beans (see page 73,
steps 1 to 6)

4 cups (1 L) **water**

One 28-oz (796-mL) can **plum
tomatoes** with juice*

4 cups (1 L) coarsely chopped
Savoy cabbage

½ cup (125 mL) **diced zucchini**

¼ tsp (1 mL) **dried basil**

---

*See pages 31 to 33 for the
substitution chart that lists
convenience foods and SCD
alternatives.

1. Heat the oil in a large pot and add the onion, carrot, and garlic. Cook and stir over medium heat for about 5 minutes.

2. Add the remaining ingredients.

3. Cook uncovered until the vegetables are tender and the soup is thick, approximately 20 minutes.

Roasted Cauliflower with Celeriac

Serves 4

This side dish is a great substitute for potatoes. The recipe can easily be doubled if you have a large enough cookie sheet or casserole dish. Be aware that baking cauliflower reduces its mass significantly.

1. Heat the oven to 350°F (180°C).

2. Wash the cauliflower and cut it into small florets.

3. Cut away the roots and hairy parts from the celeriac. Cut into small cubes.

4. Toss the celeriac and cauliflower with the olive oil and sprinkle liberally with salt.

5. Place on a large cookie sheet with sides or in a 9- x 13-inch (3.5-L) glass casserole dish.

6. Bake for 1 hour or more until browned to your liking.

7. Serve warm.

1 **head cauliflower**

1 **bulb celeriac**

1 Tbsp (15 mL) **olive oil**

Kosher salt

Latkes

Makes 1 to 2 dozen

Chanukah, the Jewish festival of lights, was always a dilemma for us. Potato latkes, the traditional food eaten during Chanukah, are forbidden while following the Specific Carbohydrate Diet. However, it didn't take much experimentation to find the right combination of alternative vegetables that produce the familiar latke consistency and, more importantly, taste. The secret to our latkes is cauliflower, a vegetable that when steamed and mashed has a taste and texture remarkably similar to potatoes. These latkes produce something that we think rival the old ones and make them taste like...well, old potatoes! We know you'll enjoy these latkes—they're not just for Chanukah anymore.

3 cups (750 mL) shredded **zucchini**

1 medium-sized **cauliflower**

1 **white onion**, chopped

Oil for frying

2 **eggs**, beaten

Salt and **black pepper** to taste

1. Place the zucchini in a tea towel and twist. Wring out as much water as you can.

2. Cut the cauliflower into florets and steam until soft. Drain, cool, and mash.

3. Squeeze the liquid from the cauliflower as you did with the zucchini.

4. Heat a bit of oil in a medium frying pan over low heat. Add the onions and cook until caramelized, about 5 to 10 minutes.

5. Combine the zucchini, cauliflower, and onions in a bowl. Add the eggs, salt, and pepper.

6. Mix with your hands to blend evenly.

7. Place a non-stick frying pan over medium heat and add enough oil to cover the bottom. When it's hot, spoon the mixture in by heaping tablespoons (15 mL). Remember, the only ingredient in this recipe that has to be cooked is the egg, so they don't have to cook for long. Turn them over when browned to your liking.

8. These can be made ahead of time and reheated uncovered in a 250°F (120°C) oven.

9. Serve with Yogurt* and/or applesauce*.

Variations: Mushroom Latkes

Add 5 thinly sliced, medium-sized mushrooms. Cook them with the onions and add them to the cauliflower and zucchini mixture.

Baked Latkes

If you don't want to deep-fry these latkes, the entire mixture can be baked in a large loaf pan or muffin tins at 350°F (180°C) for 20 minutes. They're delicious either way.

* See pages 31 to 33 for the substitution chart that lists convenience foods and SCD alternatives.

Spaghetti Squash

Serves 4 to 6

As we mentioned in Notes from the Kitchen, almond flour's only flaw is that you can't make pasta with it. Fortunately, there are many pasta substitutes if you're trying to avoid grain, and spaghetti squash is one of them. You can cook your squash and store it in the refrigerator for up to 4 days. It reheats well in the microwave.

1 **spaghetti squash**

Any of the following toppings:
salt and **butter**; **Parmesan cheese**; **tomato sauce**; **basil**, **oregano**, **salt**, and **black pepper**; **Yogurt***; **honey** and **cinnamon**; **The World's Best Meat Sauce** (page 100)

* See pages 31 to 33 for the substitution chart that lists convenience foods and SCD alternatives.

1. Cut the squash in half. Do not remove the seeds.

2. Place the pieces cut-side down in a 10- x 15-inch (4-L) casserole dish.

3. Pour in enough water to fully cover the bottom of the dish.

4. Bake for 50 to 60 minutes at 375°F (190°C) or until the squash pieces feel a bit soft when you press down on them.

5. Turn the squash pieces cut-side up and, using an oven mitt to protect your hands from the hot squash, scoop out the seeds with a spoon.

6. Use a fork to scrape out the flesh of the squash, which will come away in strands—just like spaghetti!

7. Mix with any of the toppings listed.

Quick Cook!

You can cook squash quickly in the microwave. Depending on the size of your microwave, you may have to cook half at a time. Place the squash cut-side down on a microwave-safe plate and add enough water to cover the surface of the plate. Cook on high for 8 to 15 minutes or until the squash feels a bit soft when you press down on it. Continue as for oven-baked squash.

MAIN DISHES

Eggs • Beef • Poultry • Fish and Seafood

It's surprising how many people are afraid to improvise with food. Just because a recipe calls for certain ingredients doesn't mean you have to use them all. If a stew calls for carrots, but you don't like carrots, just substitute your favourite vegetable. The trick to adapting recipes is to make sure you substitute wet ingredients for other wet ingredients, and dry ingredients for other dry ingredients. In other words, don't use a liquid, such as tomato juice, instead of carrots.

Many of the recipes in this section were created through our own substitutions. As in all our recipes, we eliminated ingredients such as refined sugar, flour, and starch. Bread crumbs in burgers are replaced with almond flour, and stews are left to thicken on their own simmer power. Vegetables and seafood are disguised as noodles, while combinations of herbs and spices bring you the tastes you love.

We've included eggs in this section because they're so versatile and give you the option of a lighter meal.

Eggs

Green Eggs

Serves 1

You can do so much with eggs. This is just one variation on a basic omelette. Sprinkle with salt, pepper, or more cheese to serve. If you have any left over, store in the refrigerator and eat it cold in a sandwich on bread (pages 132–34).

1. Oil an omelette pan, add the zucchini, onion, garlic, and pepper, and cook on medium heat for about 5 minutes.

2. Pour the eggs over the ingredients in the pan and cook until slightly brown on the bottom and slightly set on the top.

3. Sprinkle the cheese on the uncooked side of the omelette. Then flip it to cook the other side (see Easy Flipping, page 93).

Oil for frying

⅓ cup (75 mL) grated **zucchini**

2 Tbsp (25 mL) diced **onion**

½ **garlic clove**, finely diced

⅛ tsp (0.5 mL) **black pepper**

2 **eggs**, beaten

2 Tbsp (25 mL) grated **Parmesan cheese**

Variation: Squash Omelette

Substitute Spaghetti Squash (page 78) for the zucchini in this recipe and add one shake of paprika in step 1. It's a perfect way to get rid of leftover squash.

Egg Fiesta
Serves 1

This egg treat has a lot of zip. You can eat it as a scramble or an omelette. Store leftovers in the refrigerator for a cold sandwich the next day.

Oil for frying

1 stalk **bok choy,** diced

2 Tbsp (25 mL) diced **onion**

3 Tbsp (45 mL) **Tomato Paste***

2 **eggs**, beaten

1 Tbsp (15 mL) **water**

Parmesan cheese, grated

Salt, **black pepper**, and
   paprika to taste

*See pages 31 to 33 for the substitution chart that lists convenience foods and SCD alternatives.

1. Oil an omelette pan, add the bok choy, onion, and 2 Tbsp (25 mL) of Tomato Paste, and cook on medium heat until the vegetables are soft, about 5 minutes.

2. Beat the eggs, water, and the remaining 1 Tbsp (15 mL) Tomato Paste in a bowl.

3. Pour the egg mixture over the cooked vegetables in the pan.

4. Cook as an omelette (see Easy Flipping, page 93) or scramble. Sprinkle with Parmesan cheese, salt, pepper, and paprika before serving.

The World's Best Meat Sauce with Spaghetti Squash

Salmon with Sesame-Ginger Marinade

Western Omelette

Serves 2

This is a hearty meal for two, but it can easily be doubled or halved. Use plum tomatoes when in season. For best results, make the omelettes individually, using 3 eggs and half the sauce. Peeling tomatoes and peppers is simple using the technique described below.

1. Heat a bit of oil in a medium-sized frying pan on medium heat. Add the onion and sauté until caramelized, about 5 to 10 minutes.

2. Add the tomatoes and all the bell peppers, stirring for 1 minute to combine the flavours.

3. Add the tomato juice and stir.

4. Add the hot pepper sauce if desired, and season with salt and black pepper.

5. Oil an omelette pan on medium heat, and add 3 of the beaten eggs.

6. When the first side is almost set, flip over (see Easy Flipping, page 93). Place ¼ of the sauce on top of the omelette.

7. Fold over and slide onto a plate.

8. Serve with another ¼ of the sauce on top.

9. Repeat for the second omelette.

Olive oil for sautéing

1 **onion**, chopped

3 **plum tomatoes**, peeled and chopped

1 **red bell pepper**, roasted, peeled, and chopped

1 **green bell pepper**, roasted, peeled, and chopped

1 **jalapeño pepper**, roasted, peeled, and chopped

½ cup (125 mL) **tomato juice**

Salt and **black pepper** to taste

Hot pepper sauce to taste (optional)

6 **eggs**, or the equivalent combination of eggs and egg whites, beaten

Peeling Tomatoes and Peppers

To peel tomatoes, score the bottom with an "X" and place in boiling water for 30 to 60 seconds, until the skin begins to blister and fall away. Remove and plunge into a bowl of cold water. Peel off the skin and discard. **To peel peppers**, roast in a 400°F (200°C) oven until browned and blistered. Place in a closed paper or plastic bag for 5 minutes to let them sweat. Peel off and discard the skins.

Cheese Blintzes

Makes 8 blintzes

Blintzes, or sweet cheese-filled crêpes, are typically made with a flour-based batter and a sweet cottage-cheese filling. This recipe calls for the same sweetened cheese filling, but the crêpe is made solely of egg. We use Yogurt Cheese* instead of cream cheese because it has no additives and virtually no lactose.

Crêpes

3 extra-large **eggs**

½ cup (125 mL) **egg whites**

2 Tbsp (25 mL) **water**

Butter, **oil**, or **non-stick spray**

---

*See pages 31 to 33 for the substitution chart that lists convenience foods and SCD alternatives.

Crêpes

1. Crack the eggs into a large bowl, and whisk together with the egg whites and water.

2. Grease an 8-inch (20-cm), non-stick omelette pan and place over medium heat.

3. Pour 3 Tbsp (45 mL) of the egg mixture (use a ¼-cup/50-mL measure and fill it ¾ of the way full) into the pan, and swirl it around to evenly coat the bottom of the pan. Cook until the egg sets on top.

4. Flip the crêpe over and briefly cook on the second side.

5. When cooked, remove and stack on a plate.

6. Repeat until all the egg is used up. You should have 8 crêpes.

7. The crêpes can be made one day in advance and refrigerated until you are ready to fill and serve.

Filling and Assembling

1. Preheat the oven to 325°F (160°C).

2. Place cottage cheese, Yogurt Cheese, egg, vanilla, and honey into a blender or work bowl of a food processor and mix well.

3. Refrigerate the mixture for 30 minutes.

4. Place ¼ cup (50 mL) of filling in the middle of each crêpe. Fold two opposite sides of the crêpe into the centre, making a rectangle.

5. Place the blintzes fold-side down in a baking dish and dot each with a bit of butter.

6. Bake for 20 to 30 minutes until puffed up and golden brown.

Variation: Blintz Pie

Instead of separate blintzes, you can make one large blintz pie. Grease the bottom and sides of a 9-inch (1.5-L) pie plate. Layer half the crêpes on the bottom of the pie plate, overlapping if necessary. Pour the cheese mixture on top of the crêpes. Cover with the remaining crêpes, and gently brush or drizzle the top with melted butter. Bake for 30 minutes until set and golden brown. Slice and serve.

Filling and Assembling

1 cup (250 mL) **dry-curd cottage cheese** (see page 55)

1 cup (250 mL) **Yogurt Cheese**＊

1 extra-large **egg**

½ tsp (2 mL) **pure vanilla extract**

2 Tbsp (25 mL) warmed **honey**

Butter

＊See pages 31 to 33 for the substitution chart that lists convenience foods and SCD alternatives.

Zucchini-crusted Quiche Lorraine

Serves 4 to 6

Serve this quiche with a salad for a perfect lunch or light dinner. The zucchini-Parmesan crust is a great substitute for typical pastry. Its savoury flavour complements the traditional ingredients in this dish.

Crust

2 large **zucchinis**, peeled and grated

1 **egg**

½ cup (125 mL) grated **Parmesan cheese**

Bit of **butter**

Filling

4 **eggs**

1 cup (250 mL) **Yogurt***

½ tsp (2 mL) **salt**

Pinch **nutmeg**

Pinch **cayenne** pepper

Pinch **black pepper**

½ lb (250 g) chopped frozen **spinach**, thawed, and drained

5 oz (150 g) **Swiss cheese**, grated

5 oz (150 g) **cheddar cheese**, grated

*See pages 31 to 33 for the substitution chart that lists convenience foods and SCD alternatives.

Crust

1. Heat the oven to 350°F (180°C).

2. Gather the grated zucchini in a tea towel and squeeze out all the excess moisture. You'll be left with approximately 2 cups (500 mL) of zucchini.

3. Mix the zucchini, egg, and cheese together. Press into a lightly buttered 9-inch (23-cm) or 10-inch (25-cm) pie plate.

4. Bake for 20 to 30 minutes, until cooked through and lightly browned around the edges.

Filling

1. Increase the oven temperature to 450°F (230°C).

2. Beat the eggs, Yogurt, salt, nutmeg, cayenne pepper, and black pepper just long enough to thoroughly mix.

3. Place the spinach on top of the cooked zucchini crust.

4. Layer both cheeses on top of the spinach.

5. Pour the Yogurt-egg mixture on top.

6. Bake for 10 minutes. Reduce the temperature to 350°F (180°C) and bake until the filling is set (20 to 30 minutes). Insert a knife in the centre; if it comes out clean, the filling is set.

Apple Pancakes

Makes 1 serving

They say that necessity is the mother of invention. This recipe is proof positive of that. While away on vacation, Jodi grew tired of the vegetable and cheese omelette that she was eating each day while eyeing jealously the sweet pancakes and waffles others were having. One morning she took matters into her own hands. She handed the cook at the omelette station a sliced apple and asked her to make an omelette with it. She eyed Jodi dubiously. Jodi pressed on, promising her that it would be delicious. And it was—so delicious that she ate it every morning for the next week of her holiday. Double and triple this recipe as needed, but make each pancake individually and place in a 200°F (95°C) oven to keep warm until you're ready to serve.

1. Using your hands, squeeze some of the juice from the grated apple.

2. Beat the eggs in a bowl. Add the apple and cinnamon, and stir to combine.

3. Grease an 8-inch (20-cm), non-stick omelette pan over medium heat.

4. Pour the mixture into the pan.

5. While the mixture is still liquid, use a spatula to gently pull back the sides of the pancake encouraging the wet mixture to flow under the part that has already set. This will help to make a fluffier, more evenly cooked pancake.

6. When the pancake is nicely browned on the bottom, but still wet on the top, flip it over to cook the other side (see sidebar).

7. Cook the second side until done and slide it onto a serving plate.

8. The toppings for this dish are endless, but here are just a few possibilities: warmed honey, warmed berries, Strawberry Jam* (page 189), Yogurt*, jam mixed with Yogurt, Caramel Sauce (page 188), and natural peanut butter.

1 **apple**, peeled, cored and coarsely grated

2 **eggs** or ½ cup (125 mL) egg white, or combination of the two

1 tsp (5 mL) **ground cinnamon**

Butter, **oil**, or **non-stick spray**

Topping of choice

Easy Flipping

If you have trouble flipping, follow these simple steps:

1. Slide the pancake or omelette onto a plate (wet side up).

2. Place the omelette pan over the plate and quickly invert.

*See pages 31 to 33 for the substitution chart that lists convenience foods and SCD alternatives.

Beef

Rainbow Stew

Serves 6 to 8

The brightly coloured vegetables—green zucchini, yellow squash, orange carrots, purple onion, and red tomatoes—give this stew its name. As it cooks, the liquid reduces to create a thick, flavourful gravy—no flour, starch, or milk required. Serve with Decadent Onion Biscuits (page 136).

1. Put the beef, carrots, onion, tomatoes, garlic, salt, pepper, and thyme in a large pot, and add enough water to cover the contents.

2. Bring to a boil, lower the heat to medium and simmer for 1 hour with the lid ajar.

3. Add the squash and simmer for 30 more minutes.

4. Add the zucchini and simmer with the lid off until the zucchini starts to look translucent and the stew is thick (15 to 20 minutes).

2 lb (1 kg) **stewing beef**, cubed

5 large **carrots**, peeled and thickly sliced

1 large **purple onion**, coarsely chopped

One 28-oz (796-mL) can **diced tomatoes** (plum or regular) with juice*

4 **garlic cloves**, finely chopped

2 tsp (10 mL) **salt**

¼ tsp (1 mL) **black pepper**

½ tsp (2 mL) **dried thyme**

½ **butternut squash**, peeled and coarsely chopped

2 **zucchinis**, coarsely chopped

* See pages 31 to 33 for the substitution chart that lists convenience foods and SCD alternatives.

Carrot-Sage Stew

Serves 4 to 6

If you love sage, you'll adore this stew. To make it thicker, simmer it longer.

2 lb (1 kg) **stewing beef**, cubed

1 **red onion**, chopped

⅛ tsp (.5 mL) **paprika**

½ tsp (2 mL) **salt**

¼ tsp (1 mL) **black pepper**

¼ tsp (1 mL) **dried basil**

1 cup (250 mL) **water**

½ cup (125 mL) **tomato juice**

2 **tomatoes**, diced

18 whole fresh **sage leaves** or
   1 tsp (5 mL) **dried sage**

6 large **carrots**, peeled and
   coarsely chopped

1 clove **garlic**, finely chopped

1. Brown the meat in a large pot over medium heat. Remove and set aside in a bowl.

2. In the same pot, cook the onion for 5 to 10 minutes until it is translucent.

3. Add the paprika, salt, pepper, basil, tomato juice, and water to the pot, and bring to a boil.

4. Add the remaining ingredients, cover and cook for 45 minutes, stirring occasionally.

Apple Harvest Stew

Serves 6 to 8

Make this stew in the fall when apples and apple cider are at their peak. If you have a sweet tooth, you'll make it over and over again. If you can't find McIntosh apples in your grocery store, feel free to use a different variety. Serve with a light salad and Quick Applesauce for dessert (see page 146).

1. Brown the meat in a large pot over medium heat in a bit of oil.

2. Sprinkle the salt, pepper, and thyme over the browned meat.

3. Pour the cider, vinegar and water into the pot, and simmer covered for 45 minutes.

4. Add the remaining ingredients and cook uncovered for 45 more minutes.

Oil for browning

2 lb (1 kg) **stewing beef**, cubed

1 tsp (5 mL) **salt**

¼ tsp (1 mL) **black pepper**

½ tsp (2 mL) **dried thyme**

2 ½ cups (625 mL) **apple cider**

2 Tbsp (25 mL) **cider vinegar**

½ cup (125 mL) **water**

5 large **carrots**, coarsely chopped

1 **onion**, chopped

4 **stalks celery,** chopped

1 **McIntosh apple**, peeled and chopped

1 Tbsp (15 mL) **Yogurt*** (optional)

1 Tbsp (15 mL) **lemon juice**

---

* See pages 31 to 33 for the substitution chart that lists convenience foods and SCD alternatives.

Chinese Stir-fry

Serves 4 to 6

The subtle undertones of your frying oil can take a recipe from "good" to "authentic." In this dish, the peanut oil gives the stir-fry a genuine Chinese food taste. This tastes even better the next day.

3 Tbsp (45 mL) **peanut oil**

1 lb (500 g) **lean steak**, thinly sliced in long strips

Salt, **black pepper**, and **dried thyme** to taste

1 **onion**, chopped

1 **red bell pepper**, thinly sliced in long strips

1 head **bok choy**, coarsely chopped

2 large **carrots**, thinly sliced

1. Heat the oil in a wok or large frying pan over high heat. Add the beef, salt, pepper, and thyme, and sauté until brown. Remove the meat and set aside in a bowl.

2. Add the vegetables to the pan, with more salt and pepper, and sauté over high heat for 4 minutes. The vegetables will still be crispy.

3. Return the beef to the pan and cook to your liking.

Classic Burgers

Serves 4 to 6

The trick to making sensational burgers is to add moisture in the form of eggs or tomato juice and to use the right spice mix. The natural oils in the almond flour also help keep these burgers moist while grilling. Top them with the classic tomato, onion, and lettuce, or eat them plain. Try substituting ground chicken or turkey for the beef, and using grilled portobello mushrooms as buns.

1. Mix the onion, salt, juice, eggs, mustard, and almond flour in a bowl.

2. Add the beef and combine thoroughly. If the mixture is a bit too moist or loose, put it in the refrigerator for about 20 minutes before grilling.

3. Form into patties and grill for 5 to 6 minutes on each side, or until fully cooked (see below).

⅓ cup (75 mL) finely diced **onion**

¾ tsp (4 mL) **salt**

2 Tbsp (25 mL) **tomato juice**

2 **eggs**

1 tsp (5 mL) **Dijon mustard**

½ cup (125 mL) **almond flour**

1 lb (500 g) **ground beef**

Well Done, Please

You can't tell whether meat is fully cooked by how it looks. Cooked meat that appears brown isn't necessarily done, just as cooked meat that is still pink may be safe to eat. Using a food thermometer is the best way to make sure your food won't be contaminated with harmful bacteria, such as *E. coli*. Ground beef should always be cooked to an internal temperature of 160°F (71°C). Ground chicken and turkey, as well as whole pieces, should be cooked to an internal temperature of 185°F (85°C).

The World's Best Meat Sauce

Serves 6 to 8

This sauce is very meaty and chunky. To make it less meaty, add an additional 1 or 2 cans of crushed tomatoes. Use Vidalia onions when they're in season—they add a little sweetness to this savoury sauce. Serve it over Spaghetti Squash (page 78) with grated Parmesan cheese or as a sloppy Joe over any of our breads (pages 132–34).

2 lb (1 kg) **ground beef**

One 28-oz (796-mL) can **diced tomatoes** with juice*

½ cup (125 mL) **water**

1 tsp (5 mL) **salt**

1 tsp (5 mL) **dried oregano**

1 tsp (5 mL) **dried basil**

½ tsp (2 mL) **black pepper**

½ tsp (2 mL) **dried thyme**

1 large **red bell pepper**, coarsely chopped

1 large **onion**, coarsely chopped

1 large **carrot**, coarsely grated

1 large **zucchini**, coarsely grated

2 **garlic cloves**, pressed

* See pages 31 to 33 for the substitution chart that lists convenience foods and SCD alternatives.

1. In a large pot, cook the ground beef until browned. Drain away the fat.

2. Add the rest of the ingredients to the beef and simmer with the pot half-covered for 45 minutes or until the sauce is thick. Stir occasionally.

Meatloaf

Serves 6 to 8

There's no avoiding it—meatloaf sounds boring. Maybe you associate it with other childhood culinary traumas, such as having to eat your vegetables. But we promise that our meatloaf, packed full of flavour, will become one of your favourites. If you like, make it with ground chicken or turkey instead of beef. Serve it with bread (pages 132–34), a salad (pages 64–66), or a side dish (pages 75–78). Use Vidalia onions when they're in season—they add a little sweetness to this loaf.

1. Heat the oven to 350°F (180°C). Line a 9- x 5-inch (2-L) loaf pan with parchment paper.

2. Mix the onion, celery, red pepper, garlic, almond flour, salt, black pepper, mustard, Parmesan cheese, ¼ cup (50 mL) of the tomato sauce, and the eggs together.

3. Add the beef and mix well.

4. Put the mixture in the loaf pan.

5. Coat the top of the loaf with the remaining ¼ cup (50 mL) tomato sauce and sprinkle with paprika.

6. Bake for 1 hour and 10 minutes. Allow it to set by cooling slightly before cutting and serving.

½ cup (125 mL) chopped **onion**

½ cup (125 mL) chopped **celery**

½ cup (125 mL) chopped **red bell pepper**

1 **garlic clove**, finely diced

½ cup (125 mL) **almond flour**

½ tsp (2 mL) **salt**

¼ tsp (1 mL) **black pepper**

1 tsp (5 mL) **Dijon mustard**

½ cup (125 mL) grated **Parmesan cheese**

½ cup (125 mL) **Tomato Sauce***

2 **eggs**

1 lb (500 g) lean **ground beef**

Paprika

*See pages 31 to 33 for the substitution chart that lists convenience foods and SCD alternatives.

Poultry

Chicken Sausage Patties

Serves 6

For breakfast, lunch, or dinner, have these sausage patties with eggs and enjoy a hearty meal full of protein and vitamins.

1. Combine everything but the chicken in a bowl and mix well.

2. Add the chicken and mix thoroughly.

3. Form into patties and grill on each side for 5 or 6 minutes, or until the meat is fully cooked (see Well Done, Please, page 99).

1 small **Golden Delicious** or **McIntosh apple**, peeled and coarsely grated

2 Tbsp (25 mL) finely chopped **fresh sage**

¼ tsp (1 mL) **ground allspice**

1 tsp (5 mL) **salt**

¼ tsp (1 mL) **black pepper**

2 **eggs**

½ cup (125 mL) **almond flour**

1 Tbsp (15 mL) **honey**

1 tsp (5 mL) **tomato juice**

1 lb (500 g) **ground chicken**

Wasaga Burgers

Serves 6 to 8

These burgers are so tasty that you can eat them plain. However, if you just can't have a burger without toppings, add slices of mild onion, tomato, and fresh romaine lettuce or spinach. Try Decadent Onion Biscuits (page 136) for a bun.

2 **eggs**

½ cup (125 mL) **almond flour**

2 Tbsp (25 mL) finely chopped **coriander** or **parsley**

½ cup (125 mL) thinly sliced **green onions**

1 **garlic clove**, minced

1 tsp (5 mL) **salt**

¼ tsp (1 mL) **black pepper**

Pinch **paprika**

¼ tsp (1 mL) **Dijon mustard**

1 lb (500 g) **ground chicken**

1. Combine everything but the chicken and mix well.

2. Add the chicken and mix thoroughly.

3. Form into patties and grill for 5 to 6 minutes on each side, or until fully cooked (see Well Done, Please, page 99).

Seven-layer Lasagna

Makes one 9- x 13-inch (3.5-L) lasagna

This lasagna is so easy to make and tastes like the real deal. Instead of pasta noodles, it calls for thinly sliced zucchini. Once all the other ingredients are layered, you won't taste the difference between it and lasagna loaded with pasta. The recipe calls for ground chicken, but you can substitute ground beef.

1. In a large pot on medium heat, brown the ground chicken. Drain the fat. (You can use oil for browning if you wish. However, the chicken gives off enough fat that adding oil to the pot is not necessary.)

2. Add the mushrooms, garlic, oregano, basil, bay leaves, paprika, and red pepper flakes to the pot and stir well. Continue cooking until the mushrooms cook down.

3. Stir in the tomato juice and season with salt and pepper. Turn off the heat.

4. Preheat the oven to 450°F (230°C).

5. Cover the bottom of a 9- x 13-inch (3.5- L) lasagna dish with half the zucchini slices. Pour half the meat sauce on top of the zucchini. Sprinkle half the provolone on top of the sauce.

6. Repeat the layers and sprinkle Parmesan cheese over the top.

7. Bake for 45 minutes to 1 hour, until it is bubbly and the cheese on top is crispy and browned to your liking.

8. Remove from the oven and let sit for 5 minutes before serving.

9. Cut the lasagna and use a slotted spatula to serve it. Zucchini produces a bit of liquid when it cooks, and the slotted utensil allows the excess water to drain off.

1 lb (500 g) **ground chicken**

4 cups (1 L) finely chopped **mushrooms**

2 **garlic cloves**, pressed

1 tsp (5 mL) **dried oregano**

1 tsp (5 mL) **dried basil**

2 **bay leaves**

Pinch **paprika** (optional)

Pinch **red pepper flakes** (optional)

2 cups (500 mL) **tomato juice**

Salt and **black pepper** to taste

6 medium **zucchini**, peeled and sliced lengthwise into 4 to 6 slices each

1 lb (500 g) **provolone cheese**, grated

⅓ cup (75 mL) grated **Parmesan cheese**

Tacos

Serves 4 to 6

Tacos without shells—never! Tacos without corn or wheat tortilla shells—yes! The shells for these tacos are made from cheese, and they're delicious. Provolone cheese is best for this recipe because the sliced provolone is already in rounds, so it takes all the work out of making the taco shells.

Cheese Shells

12 **provolone cheese** slices
  (1 slice makes 1 shell)

Cheese Shells

1. Heat the oven to 350°F (180°C).

2. Line a cookie sheet with parchment paper.

3. Place 4 slices of provolone cheese on the parchment paper and bake for 10 minutes until the edges are crispy (the centre can still be soft), the rest is lightly browned, and you are able to lift the cheese from the parchment paper without it dripping or falling apart.

4. While the shells are baking, find a long, round utensil that you can drape the cheese rounds over to let them harden into half-moon shapes. A broom handle is perfect for this. Try to rig the broom so that it's suspended between two chairs in your kitchen. Drape paper towel over the suspended broom handle—it will absorb the grease from the cheese and give you a clean working surface.

5. Remove the cheese rounds from the oven and immediately drape them over the broom handle. You have to work quickly or the shells will harden flat. Remove the shells from the broom handle once they have hardened, approximately 2 minutes.

6. Repeat with the remaining slices.

Filling

1. In a large saucepan over medium heat, brown the ground meat with the garlic until cooked. Drain off the fat.

2. Add the tomato juice and heat through.

3. Season with salt and pepper to taste.

4. Fill the hardened cheese taco shells with the chicken mixture and top with your choice of condiments.

Filling

2 lb (1 kg) **ground chicken** or **beef**

2 **garlic cloves**, pressed

½ cup (125 mL) **tomato juice**

Salt and **black pepper** to taste

Any or all of the following:
tomato juice, chopped tomatoes, chopped onions, shredded lettuce, grated cheddar cheese, Yogurt*

---

*See pages 31 to 33 for the substitution chart that lists convenience foods and SCD alternatives.

Stuffed Sweet Peppers

Serves 4

The sweet peppers in this recipe are a perfect contrast to the savoury and spicy chicken stuffing. Cutting an "X" in the bottom of the peppers before baking allows the liquid from the pepper and the fat from the chicken to drain away into the pan while cooking. Serve these with your favourite mustard or hot sauce.

1 Tbsp (15 mL) **olive oil**

1 **large onion**, finely chopped

8 medium **bell peppers**
(red, yellow, and/or orange)

1½ lb (750 g) **ground chicken**

3 **plum tomatoes**, chopped

3 **large garlic cloves**, pressed

1 cup (250 mL) peeled and grated **zucchini**

2½ tsp (12 mL) **salt**

1 tsp (5 mL) **black pepper**

2 tsp (10 mL) **dried oregano**

½ tsp (2 mL) **red pepper flakes**

½ cup (125 mL) grated **Parmesan cheese**

1. Preheat the oven to 350°F (180°C).

2. Heat the olive oil in a small pan over medium heat and brown the chopped onion. Set aside to cool.

3. Wash and dry the bell peppers and slice off the tops. Remove the seeds and white membrane. Cut an "X" in the bottom of each pepper.

4. In a large bowl, combine the onion, chicken, tomatoes, garlic, zucchini, salt, pepper, oregano, and red pepper flakes.

5. Stuff the peppers with the chicken mixture and place them in a baking dish.

6. Bake for 55 minutes. Remove from the oven, sprinkle with Parmesan cheese and return to the oven for 5 more minutes to melt the cheese.

Spiced Honey Chicken
Serves 6 to 8

This dish brings a touch of Morocco to your table. To cut the sweetness, reduce the amount of honey you use or add more yogurt. The leftovers are perfect cold or reheated.

1. Preheat the oven to 350°F (180°C).

2. Combine the honey, garlic, yogurt, lemon rind, and lemon juice in a bowl.

3. Place the chicken skin-side up in a 10- x 15-inch (4-L) casserole dish. Drizzle half of the honey-Yogurt mixture over the meat.

4. Sprinkle with the salt, pepper, nutmeg, cloves, almonds, and raisins.

5. Place the cinnamon sticks evenly around the casserole dish.

6. Pour the rest of the honey-Yogurt mixture over the chicken and spices.

7. Bake for 1 hour and 30 minutes or until done (see Well Done, Please, page 99), basting every 20 to 30 minutes. When the meat starts to brown, flip the chicken pieces.

8. Remove from the oven and baste with the sauce before serving.

½ cup (125 mL) **honey**

2 **garlic cloves**, pressed

2 Tbsp (25 mL) **Yogurt**∗

1 tsp (5 mL) **grated lemon rind**

1 Tbsp (15 mL) **lemon juice**

3 to 4 lb (1.5 kg to 2 kg) **chicken pieces**

Salt, black pepper, ground nutmeg, and **ground cloves** for sprinkling

1 cup (250 mL) **almond slivers**

1 cup (250 mL) **raisins**

6 **cinnamon sticks**

∗ See pages 31 to 33 for the substitution chart that lists convenience foods and SCD alternatives.

Sweet and Sour Chicken Wings

Makes 20 whole wings or 40 pieces

This recipe is great on the barbecue or baked in the oven. If you choose to barbecue, baking the chicken in the oven first will ensure that the chicken is cooked through. The secret to these finger-licking wings is that they're coated in sauce before they're cooked *and* tossed in sauce after cooking.

20 whole **chicken wings**

1 cup (250 mL) **Sweet and Sour Barbecue Sauce** (page 43), divided

1. Heat the oven to 350°F (180°C).

2. Wash the chicken wings and dry them well. Remove the wing tips, and split the wings into flats and drumettes if desired.

3. Toss the raw wings with ½ cup (125 mL) of the sauce and place them in a 9- x 13-inch (3.5-L) lasagna dish in the oven.

4. If you're finishing the wings on the barbecue, bake for 30 minutes, then place on a grill at medium heat until fully cooked and coloured to your liking, about 15 minutes. For the oven method, bake for 45 minutes, turning when brown, then switch the oven to broil. Continue to cook until the wings are fully cooked and browned to your liking, approximately 10 to 15 minutes.

5. Remove the wings from the oven or barbecue, place in a large bowl and add the remaining ½ cup (125 mL) sauce. Toss until evenly coated. These wings are great hot or cold.

Quick Chicken with Peanut Sauce

Serves 4 to 6

Just because you don't eat rice doesn't mean you can't have Asian-style food. Try using Spaghetti Squash (page 78) with this dish as a rice alternative.

Sauce

1. Combine all the ingredients in a small pot. Cook over medium heat until the sauce is blended smoothly and starts to bubble. Set aside.

Chicken and Vegetables

1. Heat the olive oil and garlic in a wok or large saucepan over high heat.

2. Add the onion, carrot, and tomato. Sauté on medium heat for 5 minutes.

3. Add the meat and sauce. Cook and stir constantly until the chicken is cooked through.

4. Add the zucchini and cook until soft, approximately 5 minutes.

Check Your Zucchini

Take a taste of your zucchini before slicing it—if the peel is bitter, remove it before adding it to the stir-fry. If it's not bitter, keep the peel on to add flavour, texture, and colour.

Sauce

½ cup (125 mL) unsalted and unsweetened **peanut butter**

2 Tbsp (25 mL) **rice vinegar**∗

2 Tbsp (25 mL) **honey**

¼ tsp (1 mL) **salt**

¼ tsp (1 mL) **black pepper**

⅓ cup (75 mL) **Tomato Paste**∗

½ cup (125 mL) **water**

Chicken and Vegetables

2 Tbsp **olive oil**

2 **garlic cloves**, finely chopped

1 **Vidalia** or **Spanish onion**, coarsely chopped

4 to 5 large **carrots**, thinly sliced

1 **tomato**, thinly sliced

1 lb (500 g) **chicken** or **turkey breast**, thinly sliced in long strips

3 cups (750 mL) thinly sliced **zucchini**

∗ See pages 31 to 33 for the substitution chart that lists convenience foods and SCD alternatives.

Cornish Hens with Lemon, Salt, and Pepper

Serves 4

This is a simple way to prepare Cornish hen, which is a nice change from chicken. Since it's smaller, it requires less cooking time and is often moister than chicken. Depending on the size of the hens, you'll need either ½ or 1 whole hen per person.

2 to 4 **Cornish hens**, split at the backbones so they lie flat (see below)

1 ½ **lemons** per hen

Kosher salt

Black pepper

1. Heat the oven to 350°F (180°C).

2. Squeeze the juice from half a lemon over each hen, including the underside, and sprinkle both sides with salt and pepper. Bake skin-side up for 30 minutes in a non-reactive baking dish.

3. Turn the oven to broil and place the hens on the top rack. Broil until browned to your liking, approximately 5 minutes.

4. Remove from the oven, squeeze a second lemon half over each hen, and sprinkle liberally with additional salt and pepper.

5. Serve each hen with the remaining half lemon.

Variation: A Wing Thing

This method is a great way to cook any combination of chicken pieces, but it is particularly delicious with wings. Bake 20 pieces (10 whole wings) at 350°F (180°C) for 20 to 30 minutes. Remove from the oven and turn the oven to broil. Toss the wings in a bowl with the juice from 1 lemon. Sprinkle liberally with salt and pepper, and toss to coat all sides. Return to the top rack of the oven and broil for 10 minutes. Turn the wings over and broil an additional 5 minutes on the second side. Remove from the oven and sprinkle with more lemon.

Splitting Hens (Butterflying)

Butterflying a Cornish hen is simple. Place the hen breast down on a hard surface and press down on it until you feel the ribs pop. Using kitchen shears or a knife, cut down the middle of the back.

Jambalaya

Serves 4 to 6

Made with neither ham nor rice, this recipe belies its name. However, its flavour is still reminiscent of the Creole classic.

1. Heat the oven to 350°F (180°C).

2. Heat a bit of olive oil in a large saucepan over medium heat and brown the chicken on both sides. Remove from the pan and set aside.

3. Using the same pan, sauté the onion, garlic, and celery in a bit more olive oil until the onion is translucent, approximately 5 minutes.

4. Return the browned chicken to the saucepan.

5. Add the prepared beans, tomatoes with their juice, thyme, oregano, pepper, and red pepper flakes. Bring the mixture to a boil.

6. Transfer to a large casserole dish. Cover and bake for 30 minutes.

7. Remove from the oven, and add the shrimp and green pepper.

8. Return to the oven and bake uncovered for 20 minutes, until the shrimp are pink and cooked through.

9. Season with salt before serving.

Olive oil for browning

1 lb (500 g) boneless, skinless **chicken thighs**

1 **onion**, coarsely chopped

1 **garlic clove**, pressed

1 **stalk celery**, coarsely chopped

1 cup (250 mL) **white navy beans**, soaked and fully cooked (see Beans and Legumes, Easier to Digest, steps 1–6, page 73)

One 19-oz (540-mL) can **tomatoes***, chopped

½ tsp (2 mL) **dried thyme**

¼ tsp (1 mL) **dried oregano**

¼ tsp (1 mL) **black pepper**

Pinch **red pepper flakes**

½ lb (250 g) **shrimp**, peeled and deveined

1 **green bell pepper**, coarsely chopped

Salt to taste

*See pages 31 to 33 for the substitution chart that lists convenience foods and SCD alternatives.

One-pot Chicken and Sausage

Serves 6

This makes a delicious one-pot family meal. All you need to complete it is a salad, which you can throw together while the chicken and vegetables bake.

12 boneless, skinless **chicken thighs**

Salt and **black pepper**

Oil for browning

4 **spicy sausages** without sugars or fillers

1 **onion**, coarsely chopped

1 **garlic clove**, pressed

1½ cups (375 mL) **tomato juice**

6 cups (1.5 L) chopped **napa cabbage**

1 tsp (5 mL) **dried rosemary**

½ tsp (2 mL) **dried basil**

15 mini **white button mushrooms** (or very coarsely chopped larger ones)

2 cups (500 mL) **baby spinach**

1. Heat the oven to 350°F (180°C).

2. Season the chicken with salt and pepper. Heat a little oil in a large pot and brown the chicken in 2 to 3 batches.

3. When the chicken is browned on both sides, remove and place in a large casserole dish with a lid.

4. In the same pot, brown the sausages. Slice each sausage into 4 or 5 pieces and add to the casserole dish.

5. Add the onion and garlic to the pot and cook until translucent.

6. Add the tomato juice, and bring to a boil.

7. Stir in the cabbage, rosemary, and basil.

8. Cover and bake for 40 minutes.

9. Remove from the oven and turn the oven to broil.

10. Add the mushrooms and spinach to the casserole dish and stir to combine.

11. Return to the oven and continue baking uncovered for 5 minutes.

12. Remove from the oven. Taste and add salt and pepper if necessary before serving.

Three-Pepper Chili

Makes 4 to 6 large portions

This is a quick, colourful, no-bean chili that can be prepared in under an hour. It calls for ground chicken, but ground veal or beef can be substituted. Serve the chili over freshly chopped napa cabbage or romaine lettuce, and let the heat from the chili wilt the greens.

1. In a large soup pot, brown the ground chicken until cooked. Drain away the fat.

2. Stir in the oregano, paprika, and red pepper flakes.

3. Add the diced bell peppers and cook until just soft.

4. Add the mushrooms and cook until tender.

5. Add the tomato juice and season with salt and pepper. Cover and bring the chili to a boil.

6. Place the lettuce or cabbage in individual serving bowls and spoon the chili over top.

1 lb (500 g) **ground chicken**

½ tsp (2 mL) **dried oregano**

¼ tsp (1 mL) **paprika**

½ tsp (2 mL) **red pepper flakes**

2 **red bell peppers**, finely diced

2 **orange bell peppers**, finely diced

2 **yellow bell peppers**, finely diced

6 cups (1.5 L) **finely chopped mushrooms**

2 cups (500 mL) **tomato juice**

Salt and **black pepper** to taste

4 to 6 cups (1 to 1.5 L) chopped **napa cabbage** or **romaine lettuce**

Chicken Provençal on Enoki 'Pasta'

Makes 4 to 6 servings

Enoki are Japanese mushrooms that are long (about 5 inches/12 cm in length), thin and white with a tiny "button" on the top. They have a very mild, almost imperceptible, yet delicious flavour. They're the perfect imitation pasta; you can even twirl them around your fork! There is no need to precook these mushrooms. The heat from the sauce is enough to soften and cook them. Enoki are available in large supermarkets and Asian markets. They usually come prepackaged for one serving.

4 to 6 packages **enoki mushrooms** (one package per serving)

2 lb (1kg) boneless, skinless **chicken thighs**

2 Tbsp (25 mL) **olive oil**

1 cup (250 mL) chopped **onion**

6 **garlic cloves**, chopped

1 tsp (5 mL) **red pepper flakes**

4 cups (1 L) chopped fresh **plum tomatoes**

¼ cup (50 mL) **Tomato Paste***

1 cup (250 mL) **white wine**

¼ cup (50 mL) chopped **Italian parsley**

2 cups (500 mL) **tomato juice**

Salt and **black pepper** to taste

---

* See pages 31 to 33 for the substitution chart that lists convenience foods and SCD alternatives.

1. Cut the base off the mushrooms and rinse gently if necessary to remove any dirt above the root ends. Separate the strands of mushrooms and pile them into individual bowls.

2. Pound the chicken between waxed paper with a mallet or heavy frying pan to ¼-inch (5-mm) thickness.

3. Season the chicken with salt and pepper.

4. In a medium-sized frying pan, with a bit of oil, cook each piece of chicken on high heat until browned and just cooked through. Remove from the frying pan and keep warm.

5. Heat the 2 Tbsp (25 mL) oil in a large cooking pot over medium heat. Add the onions, garlic, and red pepper flakes and sauté for 5 minutes, until tender and starting to brown.

6. Add the chopped tomatoes, tomato paste, wine, and parsley. Boil for 2 minutes to cook out the alcohol.

7. Add the tomato juice and boil uncovered for 2 to 3 minutes.

8. Taste, and season with salt and pepper.

9. Slice the chicken into thin strips and add them to the sauce. Let them warm through.

10. Divide the sauce among the bowls, placing it on top of the mushroom "pasta." Serve immediately.

Variation: Seafood on Enoki 'Pasta'

Instead of chicken, use 2 lb (1 kg) frozen mixed seafood, or fresh squid, small shrimp, small scallops, clams, and mussels out of the shell. Thaw the seafood according to package directions and refrigerate it until you're ready to add it to the sauce. If using fresh seafood, slice the scallops and squid into bite-sized pieces to ensure even cooking. After adding the tomato juice (step 7), add the seafood, cover, and cook for 2 to 3 minutes until the shrimp is pink, the squid is opaque, and the rest of the seafood is cooked through. Don't overcook or the seafood will be tough. Finish as above with step 10.

Chicken Chili

Serves 6 to 8

Great for a cold winter's night, football party or potluck, this chili is no-fail. It does have some heat, but you can adjust the spiciness by reducing the paprika and cayenne pepper. Freeze it in meal-sized portions and defrost it later for a quick, healthy meal.

2 lb (1 kg) **ground chicken**

4 **onions**, chopped

3 **bell peppers** (any combination of red, yellow, or orange), chopped

2 tsp (10 mL) **salt**

2 tsp (10 mL) **cumin**

¼ tsp to ½ tsp (1 mL to 2 mL) **paprika**

¼ tsp to ½ tsp (1 mL to 2 mL) **cayenne pepper**

½ tsp (2 mL) **ground cinnamon**

½ tsp (2 mL) **red pepper flakes**

4 **garlic cloves**, pressed

3 cups (750 mL) fully cooked **navy beans** (see Beans and Legumes—Easier to Digest, steps 1–6, page 73)

One 48-oz (1.3-L) can **tomato juice**

One 28-oz (796-mL) can **plum tomatoes**, drained and coarsely chopped*

Cheddar cheese, grated, for garnish

1. In a large pot with a lid, brown the chicken on medium-high heat until cooked through. Drain off the accumulated fat.

2. Add the onions and bell peppers to the pot and cook uncovered for 5 minutes, until soft.

3. Add the salt, cumin, paprika, cayenne, cinnamon, red pepper flakes, and garlic. Stir to combine.

4. Add the beans, tomato juice and tomatoes.

5. Stir until well-combined, cover, and simmer for 45 minutes over medium-low heat.

6. Remove the lid and simmer uncovered for 15 more minutes.

7. Serve hot, garnished with grated cheese.

---

*See pages 31 to 33 for the substitution chart that lists convenience foods and SCD alternatives.

Fish and Seafood

Salmon with Sesame-Ginger Marinade

Serves 4

Check the ingredients of the marinades in any grocery store, and you'll find that they're loaded with refined sugars to sweeten, gums to thicken, and preservatives to give them shelf life. Even those that are called "honey marinades" have added corn syrup. This marinade, perfect for salmon fillets, is so simple and tasty that you'll think twice about buying the bottled stuff again.

½ cup (125 mL) **tomato juice**

1 tsp (5 mL) **sesame oil**

1 Tbsp (15 mL) **honey**

2 Tbsp (25 mL) freshly squeezed **lemon juice**

2 **garlic cloves**, smashed

2 **slices of ginger**, halved

2 tsp (10 mL) **sesame seeds**

1 **large green onion**

½ tsp (2 mL) **salt**

Four 6-to 8-oz (175- to 200-g) **salmon fillets**

1. Whisk together all the ingredients except for the salmon in a large, non-reactive bowl.

2. Add the salmon fillets and toss to coat them with the marinade.

3. Marinate in the fridge for 1 to 1 ½ hours, no more.

4. Heat the oven to 450°F (230°C).

5. Place the salmon fillets skin-side down in a casserole dish.

6. Cover with the marinade and bake for 10 minutes.

7. Increase the oven temperature to 500°F (260°C) and bake for an additional 5 minutes.

8. Remove from the oven and serve immediately with a wedge of lemon.

Baking Fish

A good rule of thumb when cooking fish is 10 minutes of cooking time per inch (2.5 cm) of thickness.

Salmon and Crab Patties

Makes about 3 dozen patties

Traditionally made with either bread crumbs or flour as a binder, these patties hold together beautifully without either. The addition of crab enhances the flavour, as does browning the onions before they're added to the batter. If you don't want to use crab, double the salmon.

1. Heat the olive oil in a frying pan over medium heat and sauté the onions until browned. Set aside.

2. Combine the salmon and crab in a mixing bowl and add the eggs.

3. Add the cooked onion, salt, and pepper. Using a fork, mash and combine well.

4. Add enough sunflower oil to cover the bottom of a frying pan and place over medium heat.

5. When the oil is hot, carefully add the mixture to the pan in heaping tablespoons (15 mL).

6. When the bottom of a patty is browned, turn it over and cook the other side.

7. Remove and drain on paper towel while you cook the remaining patties.

8. Serve with lemon wedges.

Olive oil for sautéing

2 **onions**, chopped

One 7 ½-oz (213-mL) can of **salmon**, drained

One 7 ½-oz (213-mL) can of **crab**, drained

2 **eggs**

Salt and **black pepper** to taste

Sunflower oil

Lemon wedges

Crab and Shrimp Casserole

Makes 4 servings

This dish can be made in single-serving springform pans or ramekins for an elegant presentation. More simply, it can be baked in a loaf pan, with portions spooned out. Either way, it's a flavourful dish that's easy to prepare. Serve with a wedge of lemon and your favourite steamed vegetables.

1 Tbsp (15 mL) **olive oil**

½ **red bell pepper**, finely chopped

½ **green bell pepper**, finely chopped

1½ Tbsp (22 mL) finely minced **jalapeño peppers** (optional)

Two 7½-oz (213-mL) cans **crab**, drained

4 oz (125 g) **uncooked shrimp**, shelled, deveined and chopped

3 **scallions**, thinly sliced

½ cup (125 mL) grated **Parmesan cheese**

1½ Tbsp (22 mL) freshly squeezed **lemon juice**

1 **extra-large egg**

2 Tbsp (25 mL) **Yogurt*** or **Cream Cheese***, divided

¼ tsp (1 mL) **salt**, or to taste

Black pepper to taste

* See pages 31 to 33 for the substitution chart that lists convenience foods and SCD alternatives.

1. Heat the oven to 350°F (180°C).

2. Place the olive oil in a small frying pan over low to medium heat. Add the red and green bell peppers and cook until soft.

3. Remove from the heat, add the minced jalapeño and let cool.

4. In a mixing bowl, combine the cooled peppers, crab, shrimp, scallions, ⅓ cup (75 mL) of the Parmesan cheese, and the lemon juice.

5. Gently mix in the egg, yogurt or cream cheese, salt, and pepper.

6. Spoon the mixture into a loaf pan, individual springform pans, or ramekins. Sprinkle with the remaining Parmesan cheese.

7. Bake for 40 minutes.

8. Serve hot.

Western Shrimp

Serves 4 to 6

Decadent Onion Biscuits (page 136) are the perfect accompaniment to this meal. See page 89 for an easy method for peeling tomatoes and peppers.

1. Thaw the shrimp according to the instructions on the package.

2. In a large pot, heat the olive oil on medium heat and fry the onion until browned.

3. Add the chopped tomatoes and peppers and stir for 1 minute to combine the flavours.

4. Stir in the tomato juice and bring to a slow boil.

5. Taste and add the hot pepper sauce (if desired), and salt and pepper if necessary.

6. Add the shrimp and toss them with the sauce. Cook for 3 to 5 minutes until the shrimp is pink and cooked through. Do not overcook or the shrimp will become tough.

7. Serve hot.

2 lb (1 kg) **frozen shrimp** (deveined, shelled, tail off or on)

2 Tbsp (25 mL) **olive oil**

4 **onions**, chopped

14 **plum tomatoes**, peeled and chopped

4 **red bell peppers**, roasted, peeled, and chopped

4 **green bell peppers**, roasted, peeled, and chopped

4 **jalapeño peppers**, roasted, peeled, and chopped

2 cups (500 mL) **tomato juice**

Hot pepper sauce to taste (optional)

Salt and **black pepper** to taste

Seafood Bouillabaisse

Serves 4

If you love seafood, this is the dish for you. It can be made with frozen fish and seafood, but if you can get it fresh, all the better!

20 medium or large **shrimp**

½ lb (250 g) **squid** with tentacles

12 **mussels** in the shell

½ lb (250 g) **monkfish**

½ lb (250 g) **tilapia**

Olive oil for sautéing

2 **onions**, sliced

½ tsp (5 mL) **dried basil**

½ tsp (5 mL) **dried oregano**

½ tsp (5 mL) **red pepper flakes**

2 **green bell peppers**, roasted, peeled, and chopped (see Peeling Tomatoes and Peppers, page 89)

7 **plum tomatoes** peeled and chopped (see page 89)

1 to 2 cups (250 to 500 mL) **tomato juice**

Salt and **black pepper** to taste

Hot pepper sauce (optional)

One 14-oz (398-mL) can of **baby clams** with juice

Italian parsley to garnish

1. Wash and clean the seafood and cut the monkfish and tilapia into 2-inch (5-cm) pieces. Set the fish and seafood aside.

2. Heat the olive oil in a frying pan over medium heat and sauté the onions until translucent, approximately 5 minutes.

3. Add the basil, oregano, and red pepper flakes, and stir to combine the flavours.

4. Add the peeled bell peppers and tomatoes, and 1 cup (250 mL) of the tomato juice.

5. The mixture should be thick. Let the sauce simmer over medium heat for 5 minutes, and then taste and season with salt and pepper if necessary. Add hot pepper sauce if desired.

6. Add the juice from the baby clams and a bit more tomato juice if the mixture appears too thick. Let it simmer for an additional 4 minutes.

7. Add the clams, tilapia, and monkfish. Simmer for 3 minutes, and then add the shrimp, squid, and mussels. Cook for another 3 minutes until the shrimp is pink, the mussels are open, and the squid is opaque. Do not overcook or the fish will become tough.

8. Remove from the heat and discard any mussels that have not opened.

9. Serve in large bowls, garnished with chopped Italian parsley.

Marinated Seafood Salad

Serves 4

Great on a hot summer's night as a meal over lettuce, or as one of several appetizers for company, this marinated seafood salad is full of flavour. Feel free to use packaged frozen seafood available at your local grocery store. Because the seafood needs time to marinate, this is the perfect make-ahead dish.

1. Thaw the seafood according to the instructions on the package. If using fresh seafood, slice the scallops and squid into bite-sized pieces.

2. Whisk all the other ingredients together in a non-reactive bowl.

3. Place enough water to cover the seafood in a large pot and bring it to a boil.

4. Add the seafood, stirring to make sure none of the pieces are sticking together. Bring back to a boil and cook for 2 minutes.

5. Drain the seafood and add immediately to the marinade.

6. Toss and refrigerate for at least 2 hours or overnight before serving.

2 lb (1 kg) **frozen mixed seafood**, or **fresh squid, small shrimp, small scallops, clams**, and **mussels** both out of the shell

1 Tbsp (15 mL) **olive oil**

1 Tbsp (15 mL) **water**

1 Tbsp (15 mL) **red wine vinegar**

Juice and pulp of 1 **lemon**

1 **garlic clove**, pressed

1 Tbsp (15 mL) **capers**

3 **green onions**, chopped

1 tsp (5 mL) **Dijon mustard**

Pinch **red pepper flakes**

Pinch **dried thyme**

Salt and **black pepper** to taste

Squid Pasta

Serves 4 to 6

This dish was inspired by one of chef and cookbook author Lucy Waverman's recipes. Her idea of using thinly sliced squid as a substitute for pasta is truly imaginative.

2 lb (1 kg) **squid**, tubes only (no tentacles), cleaned and wings cut off

1 Tbsp (15 mL) **olive oil**

2 **garlic cloves**, pressed

1 Tbsp (15 mL) **anchovy paste**

1 **red bell pepper**, chopped

1 **green bell pepper,** chopped

4 **plum tomatoes**, chopped

4 cups (1 L) chopped **mushrooms**

1½ cups (375 mL) **tomato juice**

Red pepper flakes

1. Slice the squid lengthwise to open the tube. Lay it flat and slice into long, thin strips that resemble noodles.

2. Heat the oil in a large saucepan on medium heat, and add the garlic and anchovy paste. Sauté for 30 seconds.

3. Add the bell peppers and sauté for 5 minutes.

4. Add the tomatoes and mushrooms, and sauté for 2 more minutes.

5. Add the tomato juice and bring to a boil.

6. Add the squid, bring back to a boil, and cook for 2 minutes until the squid loses its translucency and turns white. Do not overcook or it will become rubbery.

7. Remove from the heat, and spoon into large pasta bowls.

8. Sprinkle each serving with a pinch of red pepper flakes.

Preparing Squid

When you buy squid from a fish market, it generally comes cleaned. All you may need to do is remove the transparent spine or quill by running your finger along the inside of the tube. For Squid Pasta, you'll also have to remove the wings to give each piece of pasta a uniform shape. For other recipes, it's not necessary.

Grilled Squid with Sun-dried Tomatoes

Serves 4 to 6

Sun-dried tomatoes, rich and tangy, add depth and flavour to this quick and easy dish. However, timing is important: cook the squid and sauce simultaneously, so both are done at the same time.

1. Lay each tube of squid horizontal on a cutting board. Score the squid by making cuts ½ inch (1.3 cm) apart through the top layer of each tube, but not through the bottom.

2. Season the squid with salt and pepper.

3. Brush a grill or cast-iron pan with olive oil and heat on high.

4. When the pan or grill is smoking, add the squid. Keep an eye on it, turning to cook it evenly.

5. While the squid is cooking, heat a large skillet on high with a bit of olive oil. Add the sun-dried and fresh tomatoes, and sauté with a pinch of salt and pepper for 30 seconds.

6. Add the garlic and butter, and sauté for 1 more minute.

7. Transfer to a bowl and keep covered.

8. Continue to cook the squid until it turns opaque and curls, for a total of 5 to 7 minutes. Do not overcook or the squid will be tough and chewy.

9. Add a bit of oil to the pan used for the tomatoes and place over medium heat. Add the spinach, season with salt and pepper, and sauté until **just barely** wilted. Remove from the heat. (The spinach will continue to wilt from the heat of the squid and tomato mixture.)

10. Place the spinach on a serving plate and cover with half the tomato mixture.

11. Toss the squid quickly in a bowl with red wine vinegar, and place on top of the tomato and spinach. Top with the remaining tomato mixture and a squeeze of lemon. Serve immediately.

2 lb (1 kg) **squid**, rinsed

Salt and **black pepper**

Olive oil for sautéing

½ cup (125 mL) **sun-dried tomatoes**, chopped (in oil or dehydrated; follow directions on package to rehydrate)

6 **plum tomatoes**, peeled and chopped (see Peeling Tomatoes and Peppers, page 89)

2 **garlic cloves**, pressed

2 tsp (10 mL) **butter**

6 cups (1.5 L) **baby spinach**

2 Tbsp (25 mL) **red wine vinegar**

Lemon

BAKED GOODS AND SWEET TREATS

Savoury Baked Goods • Muffins • Cookies and Bars • Cakes and Pies
Candies, Nuts, and Sweet Condiments • Frozen Yogurt and Ice Cream

This is where almond flour really shines. It not only brings all the sinful delights of baked goods to people going grain-free, but it also adds the nutrition of almonds. These simple recipes taste as good as, or better than, their wheat-flour-based counterparts. Even if you don't like almonds, you'll love these treats because the almond flour has an almost imperceptible flavour. And, unlike many baked goods made with wheat flour, which are best eaten the same day, baked goods made with almond flour retain their moisture and are delicious days later.

Almond flour has other advantages. For example, you never have to sift it. Any large lumps can be easily broken up with a fork, and smaller lumps melt away as soon as you add wet ingredients.

Baking with almond flour is similar to baking with wheat flour in several ways. You can tell whether or not your almond-flour pastries are done if a cake tester, toothpick, or knife is inserted and comes out clean. Baking times and temperatures will vary depending on the type of oven, cookie sheet, muffin tin, or loaf pan you use, and most almond-flour recipes freeze and reheat well.

Of course, not all our desserts and snacks are made with almond flour. There are also recipes for rich candies and mouth-watering, virtually lactose-free frozen yogurt and ice cream.

One final tip: be sure to use pure vanilla extract—one that contains only water, vanilla beans, and alcohol or glycerin. Many vanilla extracts are labelled "pure" but contain additives, such as sugar and caramel. Pure vanilla is more expensive, but it makes all the difference.

Savoury Baked Goods

Almond-Butter Bread

Makes one 8- x 4-inch (1.5-L) loaf

This mild-tasting bread is perfect for French toast and sandwiches. Grill it, toast it, or eat it plain.

3 **eggs**, separated

Pinch **salt**

1 cup (250 mL) **almond butter** with no additives (mix to re-incorporate oil that gathers at the top)

1 whole **egg**

1 tsp (5 mL) **baking soda**

1. Heat the oven to 325°F (160°C). Line the bottom of an 8- x 4-inch (1.5-L) loaf pan with a piece of parchment paper.

2. Beat the egg whites with a pinch of salt until stiff, but not dry.

3. In a large mixing bowl, combine the almond butter, 3 egg yolks, 1 whole egg, and baking soda, and beat with an electric mixer. This mixture will be stiff.

4. Fold ⅓ of the egg whites into the almond-butter mixture to soften it.

5. Gently fold the remaining egg whites in two additions into the almond-butter mixture. The mixture will be thick and stiff, but try not to deflate the egg whites.

6. Pour the batter into the prepared loaf pan and bake for 30 to 40 minutes.

7. Remove from the oven and cool. Run a knife along the inside of the loaf pan to loosen the bread before removing from the pan. Cut into slices and freeze portions for easy future use.

Basic Bread

Makes one 9- x 5-inch (2-L) loaf

This basic bread may not be as fancy as some of our others, but it's still delicious. Its texture approaches that of corn bread when made with Yogurt instead of Yogurt Cheese (page 39). Eat this as a Sloppy Joe with The World's Best Meat Sauce (page 100) or make a sandwich with Meatloaf (page 101).

1. Preheat the oven to 350°F (180°C). Line a 9- x 5-inch (2-L) loaf pan with parchment paper.

2. Combine the almond flour, Parmesan cheese, baking soda, and salt in a bowl.

3. Stir together the butter, Yogurt Cheese, and eggs in another bowl.

4. Add the dry ingredients to the wet and mix well. If you've used Yogurt Cheese, the batter will be very stiff.

5. Pour into the prepared loaf pan and bake for 40 to 45 minutes if you've used yogurt. If you've used Yogurt Cheese, bake for 35 minutes.

6. Remove from the oven and cool. Run a knife along the inside of the loaf pan to loosen the bread before removing from the pan. Cut into slices and freeze portions for easy future use.

2½ cups (625 mL) **almond flour**

½ cup (125 mL) grated **Parmesan cheese**

1 tsp (5 mL) **baking soda**

½ tsp (2 mL) **salt**

2 Tbsp (25 mL) unsalted **butter**, melted

1 cup (250 mL) **Yogurt*** or **Yogurt Cheese***

2 **eggs**

---

* See pages 31 to 33 for the substitution chart that lists convenience foods and SCD alternatives.

Soufflé Bread

Makes 20 slices

The most difficult part of following a strictly grain-free diet is what to do for bread. Finding grain-free bread you love opens up a whole new realm of food. Suddenly, you can eat sandwiches, French toast, grilled cheese—you can even have a hamburger bun. All of these yearnings inspired this recipe. It's light, fluffy, and delicious on its own or toasted and used like any other bread.

9 **egg whites**

Pinch **salt**

6 **egg yolks**

⅔ cup (150 mL) **dry-curd cottage cheese** (see page 55) or **Cream Cheese***

2 Tbsp (25 mL) **water** (eliminate water if using Yogurt Cheese)

---

*See pages 31 to 33 for the substitution chart that lists convenience foods and SCD alternatives.

1. Heat the oven to 300°F (150°C).

2. Beat the egg whites with the salt until firm, stiff peaks form.

3. In a food processor or blender, mix together the remaining ingredients until well blended.

4. Gently fold the mixture into the egg whites until they are evenly combined.

5. Line a large (14- x 20-inch/35.5- x 60-cm) cookie sheet with sides with parchment paper.

6. Spread the batter evenly over the parchment paper.

7. Bake for 30 minutes.

8. Remove from the oven. While still warm, lift the bread from the cookie sheet by holding two corners of the parchment paper. Invert it onto the cookie sheet.

9. Remove the parchment paper. Return the bread to the oven and bake for an additional 10 minutes.

10. Remove from the oven. Let cool and cut into 20 squares.

Variations: Cinnamon Soufflé Bread

For cinnamon soufflé bread, add 1 tsp (5 mL) ground cinnamon and 1 tsp (5 mL) honey to the egg mixture before blending. Perfect for French toast!

Storing Soufflé Bread

Bundle the bread in groups of 4 to 6, each slice separated by a piece of plastic wrap. Put the bundles in a plastic bag or container in the freezer. Remove one bundle at a time as needed, and store in the refrigerator for up to 1 week.

Getting Creative

There are countless ways to use this bread. These are some of our favourites:

- **Grilled cheese sandwiches.** Place sliced cheese between two pieces of the bread. Butter the outsides of the bread and brown one side at a time in a skillet on medium heat. Remove when the cheese has melted.

- **Hamburger buns**. If you don't like square ones, use a crown muffin pan (a muffin pan that makes only the tops of muffins) to bake round buns.

- **French toast**. Dip slices of bread in a beaten egg or egg white and cook in a frying pan. Top with melted butter, cinnamon, warmed honey, or heated fruit—or all four!

Decadent Onion Biscuits and Crackers

Makes 20 to 24 biscuits, or 40 to 50 crackers

You won't miss "normal" bread after tasting this melt-in-your-mouth delicacy. It goes perfectly with Spaghetti Squash (page 78) and The World's Best Meat Sauce (page 100) and is excellent as a hamburger bun. You can even make it into crackers and eat them as a crunchy, savoury treat instead of potato chips.

3 cups (750 mL) **almond flour**

½ cup (125 mL) grated **Parmesan cheese**

¼ cup (50 mL) finely chopped **parsley**

1 tsp (5 mL) **dried oregano**

½ tsp (2 mL) **dried thyme**

¼ tsp (1 mL) **dried basil**

½ tsp (2 mL) **salt**

½ tsp (2 mL) **baking soda**

3 **eggs**

1 cup (250 mL) **Yogurt*** or ¾ cup (175 mL) **dry-curd cottage cheese** mixed with ¼ cup (50 mL) water (see page 55)

2 **garlic cloves**, pressed

1 small **onion**, finely diced

* See pages 31 to 33 for the substitution chart that lists convenience foods and SCD alternatives.

Biscuits

1. Heat the oven to 325°F (160°C).

2. Combine the almond flour, cheese, parsley, oregano, thyme, basil, salt, and baking soda in a bowl.

3. In another bowl, combine the eggs, yogurt or dry-curd cottage cheese and water, garlic, and onion.

4. Add the dry ingredients to the wet and mix well.

5. Spoon the batter in mounds onto a non-stick cookie sheet or one lined with parchment paper, using a heaping 2-Tbsp (25-mL) measure.

6. Bake for 15 to 18 minutes.

Crackers

1. Heat the oven to 350°F (180°C). Line a 9- x 5-inch (2-L) loaf pan with parchment paper.

2. Repeat steps 2 to 4 above.

3. Pour the batter into the prepared loaf pan and bake for 40 to 50 minutes.

4. Cool the loaf completely and refrigerate to make slicing easier. Cut it in half lengthwise and slice each half into ¼-inch-thick (6-mm) pieces.

5. Place the slices on a cookie sheet and bake at 170°F (75°C) for 2 hours, or until they are very hard.

6. Turn off the heat and let the crackers cool in the oven.

7. Store in an airtight container to maintain crispness.

Parmesan Puffs and Crackers

Makes 20 to 24 biscuits, or 40 to 50 crackers

This is another recipe for bread that can double as crackers. It's great on its own for breakfast, a snack, or a side dish.

Puffs

1. Heat the oven to 325°F (160°C).

2. Combine the almond flour, cheese, salt, basil, oregano, and baking soda in a bowl.

3. In another bowl, combine the water, eggs, yogurt, and butter.

4. Add the dry ingredients to the wet and mix well.

5. Spoon the batter in mounds onto a non-stick cookie sheet or one lined with parchment paper, using a heaping 2-Tbsp (25-mL) measure.

6. Bake for 15 to 18 minutes.

Crackers

1. Heat the oven to 350°F (180°C). Line a 9- x 5-inch (2-L) loaf pan with parchment paper.

2. Repeat steps 2 to 4 above.

3. Pour the batter into the prepared loaf pan and bake for 40 to 50 minutes.

4. Cool the loaf completely and refrigerate to make slicing easier. Cut the bread in half lengthwise and slice each half into ¼-inch-thick (6-mm) pieces.

5. Place the slices on a cookie sheet and bake at 170°F (75°C) for 2 hours, or until they are very hard.

6. Turn off the heat and let the crackers cool in the oven.

7. Store in an airtight container to maintain crispness.

3 cups (750 mL) **almond flour**

1½ cups (375 mL) grated **Parmesan cheese**

¾ tsp (4 mL) **salt**

¼ tsp (1 mL) **dried basil**

¼ tsp (1 mL) **dried oregano**

½ tsp (2 mL) **baking soda**

½ cup (125 mL) **water**

2 **eggs**

½ cup (125 mL) **Yogurt***

2 Tbsp (25 mL) unsalted **butter**, melted

* See pages 31 to 33 for the substitution chart that lists convenience foods and SCD alternatives.

Sesame-Dijon Crackers

Makes approximately 10 dozen crackers

This is an adaptation of a cracker recipe created by our friend Sue Krivel. Until we tried Sue's crackers, we didn't believe crackers could be made without grain. And after we tasted them, we knew we'd never eat a store-bought cracker again. When you put crackers out for your guests, these are always the first to disappear. The directions are very detailed, but following them carefully will ensure success. You'll require 2 paper-towel tubes to help shape this dough for freezing.

2½ cups (625 mL) **almond flour**

1¼ cups (300 mL) grated
 Parmesan cheese

¼ cup (50 mL) **sesame seeds**

½ tsp (2 mL) **salt**

½ tsp (2 mL) **black pepper**

½ tsp (2 mL) **baking soda**

¼ tsp (1 mL) **cayenne pepper**

2 **eggs**

¾ cup (175 mL) **dry-curd
 cottage cheese** (page 55)
 or **Cream Cheese***

2 Tbsp (25 mL) **Dijon mustard**

Kosher salt for sprinkling

---

*See pages 31 to 33 for the
 substitution chart that lists
 convenience foods and SCD
 alternatives.

To Make the Dough

1. Combine the almond flour, Parmesan cheese, sesame seeds, salt, black pepper, baking soda, and cayenne pepper in a large mixing bowl.

2. Blend the eggs, dry-curd cottage cheese or yogurt cheese, and mustard in a food processor, blender, or by hand until the mixture is very smooth.

3. Add the wet mixture to the dry mixture and combine well by hand.

4. Divide the dough in half and shape each half into a log. Wrap each log in plastic wrap and roll it back and forth until the log is long and narrow enough to slide into a paper towel tube.

5. Once the dough is in the tube, place your palms on either end of the tube. Shake it from side to side so the cracker dough expands to fill the space. Put the tubes in the freezer until the dough is frozen.

To Bake

1. Heat the oven to 325°F (160°C).

2. Remove one tube from the freezer and allow it to sit at room temperature until it's just soft enough to slice, but not too soft, approximately 10 minutes.

3. To slice, keep the dough in the tube, moving it out of the tube a couple of inches at a time while you slice—this will keep the batter from softening from the warmth of your hands. Slice very thinly (⅛ inch/3 mm) with a sharp, thin knife (a boning or filleting knife works well), and place on a generously buttered cookie sheet. You can place them close together—they will not spread. Sprinkle lightly with kosher salt.

4. Bake for 8 minutes.

5. Remove the pan from the oven and turn the crackers over. Sprinkle again with kosher salt and bake for another 6 minutes.

6. Remove from the oven and allow the crackers to cool on the sheet. Reduce the oven temperature to 170°F (75°C).

7. Once the crackers are cool, return them to the oven for 30 to 60 minutes, until they're entirely crisp. Turn off the heat and let the crackers cool in the oven. Multiple batches can be piled up for crisping on one tray. The reheating ensures crackers will be crisp and stay crisp while stored in an airtight container or bag.

8. Serve these crackers as you would any others, with cheese, dip, or pâté.

Gourmet Pizza
Serves 1

Even without grain, you can still enjoy a pizza. This delectable almond-flour pizza crust will make you forget about those greasy delivery pizzas. This is adapted from an ingenious recipe by John Higgins found in the book *Breaking the Vicious Cycle*. You can eat it straight out of the oven, or cold or at room temperature on the go. Slice your leftovers into pieces and toss them in your lunch bag—the whole office will be envious of your fancy, open-face sandwich. To double or triple this recipe, use 2 eggs; to quadruple it, use 3 eggs.

½ cup (125 mL) **almond flour**

1 Tbsp (15 mL) grated **Parmesan cheese**

¼ tsp (1 mL) **salt**

½ tsp (2 mL) **dried basil**

½ tsp (2 mL) **dried oregano**

¼ tsp (1 mL) **dried thyme**

1 tsp (5 mL) **olive oil**

1 **large egg**

Tomato Paste* or **Tomato Sauce***

Pizza toppings of your choice

Parmesan cheese, grated

---

* See pages 31 to 33 for the substitution chart that lists convenience foods and SCD alternatives.

1. Heat the oven to 325°F (160°C). Line a cookie sheet with parchment paper and grease with olive oil.

2. Combine the almond flour, cheese, salt, basil, oregano, thyme, olive oil, and egg in a mixing bowl. The dough will be the consistency of cookie batter.

3. Spread the dough thinly on the cookie sheet to a 6- to 8-inch (15- to 20-cm) diameter.

4. Top with tomato paste or sauce.

5. Spread on your pizza toppings and sprinkle generously with Parmesan cheese.

6. Drizzle olive oil over the pizza.

7. Bake for 18 to 20 minutes.

Make-ahead Pizza Crusts

You can make a pizza crust and freeze it for almost instant pizza. Make the dough and flatten with a rolling pin between two pieces of parchment paper or plastic wrap until it's the appropriate diameter. Make it very thin for a gourmet, thin-crust pizza. Freeze the flattened dough, still between the parchment paper or plastic wrap, in a plastic freezer bag or sealed container to prevent freezer burn. No need to thaw before baking—just add the sauce and toppings, and bake at 325°F (160°C) for 20 minutes.

Muffins